SOCIALIZATION OF WOMEN IN INDIA

About the Author

Manju Devi, M.A. and Ph.D from Banaras Hindu University, Varanasi, is currently working as a senior lecturer in the Kashi Naresh Government Post Graduate College, Gyanpur, Bhadohi. Prior to this she has been associated with many research assignments and field duties of Gandhi Vidya Sansthan's Project "Employment conditions in the unorganized sector : A study of women workers in the Readymade Textile Garment Industry". She was closely associated with the women's struggle work of the centre for women's studies and development, B.H.U. Varanasi. The centre for Social Research, New Delhi, where she worked as a co-ordinator which helped her a lot in understanding the women problems in depth.

Socialization of Women in India

MANJU DEVI
Senior Lecturer in Psychology
Kashi Naresh Government Post-Graduate College,
Gyanpur, Bhadohi

CONCEPT PUBLISHING COMPANY, NEW DELHI-110059

ISBN : 81-8069-086-5

First Published 2004

Published and Printed by
Ashok Kumar Mittal
Concept Publishing Company
A/15-16, Commercial Block, Mohan Garden
New Delhi-110059 (India)

Phones : 25351460, 25351794
Fax : 091-11-25357103
Email : publishing@conceptpub.com

Preface

"Change is the essence of progress" and development within any society. The status of women in the Indian society is in a process of change. The women are now able to lead a more independent lifestyle and have more options open to them than in the traditional society of the past years. This opening of the system has led to a temporary state of imbalance where the role expectations from women, and their pattern of socialization is, still at times, governed by the old codes of conduct even though they have newer fields open to them. How the women adopt and remain well adjusted within these situations is the focus of this research investigation. An attempt was made to compare certain need related personality aspects and self-esteem of married employed, married unemployed and single employed women in the present study.

A perspective of the changing status of women, the prevalent sex-role expectations and sex-role definitions along with certain theoretical frameworks, to understand the personality of women in employment, have been presented in Chapter 1, 'Introduction'.

In Chapter 2 a review of the available literature related to Need related personality aspects and self-esteem of employed and unemployed women have been presented. Hardly any study directly related to the chosen topic of investigation were found. But the quoted studies, if only indirectly, do throw some light on the problem under investigation.

The methodology including the description of sample, research tools, method of data collection and statistics used in investigation under report have been described in Chapter 3.

The results have been presented in tabular and graphic forms and have been analysed and discussed in Chapter 4.

A résumé of the total investigation has been presented in Chapter 5.

Manju Devi

Acknowledgements

During the period of investigation and preparation of this report, help was received from many quarters.

I express my indebtedness and gratitude to Dr. Reeta Kumar, Department of Psychology, Banaras Hindu University, who not only guided me throughout the period of my research work with her deep knowledge and insight and practical experience but also inspired confidence and patience to pursue the research work.

I am highly indebted to all the university teachers and housewives who comprise the sample for this study. They gave their valuable time and bore with me patiently during the process of data collection.

Manju Devi

Contents

1

Introduction

The women, in the contemporary society, are in the process of acquiring a status, position and role which is different from the earlier conceptions. The Indian society, like a number of classical societies has been patriarchal and the ideal women are those who do not strive to break the bonds of control. A look into the history, however, shows that the situation was not always so.

Women in Vedic Cultural had better status in terms of education, religious rights, freedom of movement etc. In the post-Vedic period, the position of women declined and there was overwhelming concern for purity and honour. The mantle of which fell on women and they were closeted within the four walls of home in the roles of wives and mothers (Desai & Krishnaraj, 1987).

During the pre-independence period, the social reform movement of nineteenth century and nationalist movement of twentieth century, both drew the women outside, the home, initially to provide support in the freedom struggle, but once drawn outside the confines of the home, this pattern continued for the women even in the post-independent era. There was greater stress on education and the number of women entering salaried, remunerative occupations and professions has kept on increasing substantially.

The census data for the literacy rates from 1941-1981 clearly shows that whereas literacy rates for females recorded in the years 1941 and 1951 were as low as 7.30 and 7.93, there was a steady increase in the following decades. The rates shot up to the levels of 12.95 in 1961, 18.69 in 1971 and 24.88 in 1981 (Tables 1.1 & 1.2).

Table 1.1 : Literacy Rates of India, 1941-1981

Year	Both sexes	Males	Females
1941	16.10	24.90	7.30
1951	16.67	24.95	7.93
1961	24.02	34.44	12.95
1971	29.45	39.45	18.69
1981	36.17	46.74	24.88

Source : P. Padmanabha, Census of India : 1981, Series I, India Paper-1 of 1981, Provisional Population Totals (New Delhi, Office of the Registrar General and Census Commissioner for India).

Table 1.2 : Literacy Rates of U.P. and Varanasi District *(Percentage)*

	Year	Persons	Males	Females
U.P.	1981	27.16	38.76	14.04
	1971	21.70	31.50	10.60
	1961	17.70	27.30	7.00
Varanasi District	1981	31.85	45.95	16.25
	1971	27.30	40.00	13.30
	1961	23.60	36.80	9.60

Source : 1961, 1971 and 1981 Census.

The percentage of growth in enrolment at various levels of education also shows that during these years the greatest increase has been at the university level (Table 1.3). In the services and professions the number of female workers has been growing

Table 1.3 : Percentage growth in enrolments by level of education

Levels of education	Percentage increase 1960/61 to 1965/1966		Percentage increase 1965/66 to 1970/71	
	Boys	Girls	Boys	Girls
Preprimary	45.00	43.90	29.90	24.80
Primary	34.90	56.10	20.60	24.20
Secondary	49.70	70.60	18.20	21.20
University	76.30	119.40	57.30	61.50
Professional and special	16.50	74.60	3.90	9.30
All levels	37.10	60.10	20.50	24.20

Source : "Towards Equality" Report of the Committee on the Status of Women, Department of Social Welfare, December, 1974.

steadily though slowly. Of these, professional women are mostly concentrated in the teaching profession.

Commenting on the increasing trend of women entering into employment, Moorthy, as early as 1945, had commented that "The increasing entry of our women into gainful occupations has broken the old world view of division of labour 'man for the field and woman for the hearth'. It has called upon women to make physical and psychological adjustments doubtfully consistent with her dignity".

Other authors, however, are less doubtful about the ability of the women to manage the two roles together. Montague writes : For a married woman to be gainfully employed outside the home is in no way incompatible with her being a good wife, millions of married working women constitute proof on the contrary.

As a result of changing values and attitudes of today's women towards careers, more and more women are rejecting the traditional housewife role and are choosing careers (Mason *et al.*, 1976).

In context to the Indian situation, Dube (1963) has pointed out that the traditional conception regarding the place and role of women are slowly changing in contemporary Indian society.

Women in India are gradually getting more concerned about employment and profession and holding more positive attitudes towards employment and have a clearer perception of the chosen occupation (Rao, 1976).

The educated women now prefer occupations out of personal interest as a vocation and not as temporary measure. Even though, initially women moved outside the home to strengthen the hands of men economically or politically, they now seek the employment not only as a economic necessity but as a means of self-fulfilment. Kapur (1974) on the basis of her survey of 300 urban women had come to the conclusion that "educated married women of urban India are impelled to get into employment or professions not only by economic insufficiency but also by various other socio-psychological motivation". (p. 13).

Kapur (1974) further states that educated urban women have now begun to realise that job can raise their self-esteem and self-confidence and can accomplish their socio-psychological security and freedom. The various studies and surveys as well as statistics show that educated women are now more keen and desirous of utilising their education and training than was the case previously.

The employed women, thus, find themselves in a role which is non-traditional and has till lately been played mostly by men. The role of the worker requires the presence of certain personality characteristics which are usually associated with masculine sex-role identity. Men from the earlier age itself are encouraged to develop these characteristics while women are discouraged.

Prevalent Sex-Role Expectations

Most societies describe and encourage the role of child bearer and rearer for the women and disapprove alternative roles such as gainful employment outside the home (Blake, 1969).

To be successful in a profession characteristics like achievement motivation, competency, assertiveness, independence, analytical thinking, self-confidence, competitiveness, having initiative etc. would be desirable but in a large number of research investigations it has been found that these very characteristics are not included within the acceptable role expectations from women.

The literature dealing with female role behaviour suggests that women are expected to be sympathetic, humanitarian, compassionate, and dependent on one another (Tyler, 1965), non-aggressive (Hilgard & Atkinson, 1967), having spiritual values, artistic inclinations and concern for the welfare of others (Miner, 1965), conversely a behavioural orientation toward power, initiative, and prestige is frequently viewed as more appropriate for males.

Bem (1974, 1975) and Broverman, Vogel, Broverman, Clarkson and Rosenkrantz (1972) concluded that sex-roles have revealed consistent expectations for different traits and behaviours for men and women. Associated with feelings of dependency, helplessness, passivity, over emotionality, and subjectivity, femininity emphasises feeling as opposed to doing. Masculinity, on the other hand is associated with independence, action aggressive tendencies, analytic thinking, and high motivation for achievement.

Rosenkrantz and his colleagues (1968) found that "competence" and "assertiveness" are socially desirable traits for males whereas "warmth" and "expressiveness" are considered to be desirable for females.

Broverman, Vogel and Broverman *et al.* (1970) report that male valued stereotypic items reflect a "competency" cluster including attributes like being independent, objectives, active, competitive, logical, skilled in business worldly, adventurous, able to make decisions, self-confident, always acting as a leader, ambitious. The female valued stereotypic items are characterised by relative absence of these traits and consist of attributes such as gentle, sensitive to the feelings of others, tactful religious, neat, quiet, interested in art and literature, able to express tender feelings. Men are stereotypically perceived as lacking in these characteristics.

The earlier socialization of a woman and the process of development of the sex-role identity would be expected to instil personality characteristics consonant with the female sex-role identity within the women. In the Indian society, the dichotomy between the female and male sex-role identity is still quite clear cut. Under these circumstances when women enter the worker role then the possibility exists that they may find the demands of the role not in consonance with their sex-role identity.

Gove (1972) and Gove and Tudor (1973) also suggest that changes in female role have promoted conflicting and contradictory normative beliefs about the women's role, resulting in greater psychological strain.

According to the role theorists like Newcomb (1965) a persons's attitudes are influenced by the "role" he occupies in a social system, with this "changed-role" of women. It is inevitable that her ways of feelings, thinking, looking at things, willing and of doing things should also be affected.

The question, thus arises as to how the women operate within these changed roles and whether their personality is affected by this change in the socio-cultural system. The present study addresses itself to this very question.

The problem has not received due attention of the researches even though some theoretical explanations do exist which throw some light on the issue.

Theoretical Approaches

In context to the women's work behaviour two approaches earlier discussed in the writings of Kanter (1975) and Stromberg and Harkess (1978) are meaningful. These two approaches are the socialization hypotheses and a social structural approach. These theoretical explanations have not been followed up by systematic research and hence, explorations in the field are lacking.

The socialization hypotheses focuses on the family centred roles of women. The women, from the earlier age, are socialized to play the family centred roles like daughter, sister, wifc and mother. Their socialization pattern lays a great stress on the fact that women have a primary commitment to these family roles and work or career can only be of secondary importance.

Family and work are considered to be separate institutions that make competing demands on women. Since, women are socialized to give priority to family roles hence, their work related behaviour is also affected. They may scale down their achievement and aspirations in order to avoid competing with potential mates (Komarovsky, 1946) or to forego demanding occupations in the interest of motherhood and marriage (Simpson and Simpson, 1961). Horner's (1968) Concept of Fear of Success also propagates the same line of argument that women may hide or lower their achievement for fear of being considered deviant from the prevalent sex-role expectations. They may also manifest other feminine sex-role related behaviour even in work situations like submissiveness, lack of autonomy, dominance or aggressive behaviours. Hence, whenever work competes with prevalent sex-role identity and family responsibilities accommodations are made in favour of the family and the sex-role identity.

The women who do not marry can escape the constraints of the family roles hence, they can perform with greater freedom in the worker role. They are free to exhibit characteristics which may be different from their sex-role identity and consonant with the worker identity. They can more easily manifest some of the masculine characters which are associated with the worker role.

It would appear that on the basis of the socialization hypotheses the married women irrespective of their career status are likely to be more similar and different from career women who have remained single.

The other approach the social structural approach explains women's work behaviour and consciousness on the basis of their work position. This approach posits that family and work situation are social structure in which persons act and behave according to the structural demands. If women appear to be exhibiting behaviours like denying presence of aspiration or need for achievement it may be not because of their earlier socialization or sex-role identity but due to their positions within the social structure.

Working women when moving out of the boundaries of home enter those areas of activity which are male dominated. Most of the women are concentrated within certain female type occupations, these occupations have secondary positions (Grim and Stern, 1974). They are characterised by limited opportunities and power (Kanter, 1975).

Women's occupations are subordinate to male ones and women accommodate to their subordination by manifesting characteristics which would meet the circumstances. Their behaviour is that of powerless and opportunityless people. Even men may behave in similar fashion if they find themselves in similar position within social structures.

Thus, in the social structural view the women's work behaviour reflects their work situations and not latent sex-identity or a competing commitment to family roles. This structural explanation is consistent with writings as diverse as those of Marx, Mannheim, Gerth and Mills and Symbolic interactionists.

The social structural hypothesis implies that women have high workers consciousness and express it when situations are relevant to their work interest.

According to this approach we should find working women irrespective of their marital status to be similar. Since both are in situation which demand a reflection of their worker identity. They both would be expected to differ from the housewives who are only playing the family role and are not faced with the situation requiring the manifestation of a worker identity.

Research is needed in order to ascertain the comparative merits of the two theoretical approaches and the present study is an attempt to fill this lacuna. In context to the employed women the most important aspect of the personality to be investigated appear to be their need patterns. It seems essential to explore as to what motivates these women and whether they differ in their need patterns from women who are not in employment. Another aspect of relevance was considered to be self-esteem as earlier sociological studies have pointed out that women may seek the employed status to enhance their self-esteem.

Relevant research literature related to these two aspects, Need-Pattern and Self-Esteem, has been presented in the next chapter.

2

Review of Literature

It may be pointed out at the outset that studies directly related to comparison of employed women and housewives on need related aspects and self-esteem are very few. In the review those studies have been included which may, if not directly then at least indirectly, throw some light on the aspects relevant to the present investigation.

Need Related Studies

Need Achievement has been the most researched aspect in context to employed women. Most of the studies including McClelland's initial elaborations of the Achievement motivation consider Achievement to be a masculine characteristics. In fact, McClelland, Atkinson, Clark and Lowell (1953) considered it to be having little applicability for females. In 1958, Atkinson published an entire volume *Motives in Fantasy, Action and Society* and it included only one footnote about women's achievement (Horner, 1969).

Horner (1968) in a different way propagated this view through the concept of fear of success which proposed to explain the problem of non-appearance of achievement related behaviour among women. The theory of fear of success presupposes the fact that women either fail to or hide the display of success oriented behaviour.

Sex-difference related studies also conclude that women are governed by socio-emotional needs whereas men are more work and achievement oriented.

Bardwick (1971) observes that college men are primarily pre-occupied with achievement whereas females are more affiliation oriented.

Robbins, Lillian *et al.* (1983) found that women were more inclined towards artistic and domestic interests and helping others; men were interested in scientific investigation, athletics and adventure.

At an earlier age itself differences in rearing patterns encourage achievement related behaviour for boys but not for girls and it is quite likely that sex-differences in need achievement may be more due to earlier socialization pattern than due to inherent differences between the sexes. If encouraged, even women are likely to become highly achievement oriented.

Winterbottom's (1958) work has shown that when early self-reliance and mastery are expected and rewarded by the parents, the child internalizes these values and is prone to develop a high achievement motive (*n*-Achievement).

In general, however, assertiveness, constructive aggression and striving for achievement and excellence all characteristics, considered desirable in adults in this society, are discouraged for women, while tenderness, emotional warmth, and expressiveness, equally valued in the abstract, are not encouraged for men (Rossi, 1964).

As a result, differences in *n*-Achievement between males and females may appear at early stages of development itself.

Horner (1972) found that by adolescence, boys are urged to do well in school and to plan for their careers, whereas achievement by girls is discouraged.

These early socializing influences, in fact, are so strong that women completely internalize these and their self-description also tends to match the prevalent views.

Ruddel (1982) found that women described themselves as less achievement oriented, less dominant and less autonomous than men but they scored higher on affiliation, harm avoidance, nurturance, order and succourance.

Another view propagated the idea that even achievement related behaviour is directed by affiliative need in women. Alper & Greenberger (1967), Veroff, Wilcox & Atkinson (1953) propose that females who do achieve do so out of need for affiliation, *i.e.* need for social and interpersonal rewards. Males are motivated to achieve, females are motivated to affiliate. As a result, they are perceived to be suffering from Achievement *vs.* Affiliation conflict (Oetzel, 1966; Walberg, 1969).

Hoffman (1972) found that males achieve because of internalized motives to do well, to strive for excellence. Females achieve, if at all, because of desire for affiliation and social approval.

Garai and Scheinfeld (1968) have also suggested that achievement behaviour in girls is not motivated by mastery striving as with boys, but by affiliative motives.

Most of these studies base their concept of Achievement goals on McClelland's initial conceptualization of Achievement motivation. In which striving for excellence usually in masculine areas of activity were recognised as presence of *n*-Achievement. This conceptualizing of Achievement goals as being purely masculine has been questioned by some authors. Women may strive for excellence but in fields other than the usual masculine pursuits.

Crandall (1963) proposed that the primary area of feminine skill, within the traditional bounds of femininity, is social skill. Many females see social situations as achievement situations. There is an expression of their achievement strivings within the feminine role. The social context of female's achievement has been misinterpreted as evidence for affiliation, as opposed to achievement motives.

Another possibility exists that women may perceive certain areas of masculine activities as less contradictory to feminine role expectations. By entering these pursuits, they may fulfil their Achievement needs without being on contradiction to their sex-role identity.

There is some evidence that females who engage in Achievement striving define Achievement in intellectual activities as more feminine than those who do not pursue these activities (Lesser, Krawitz & Packard, 1963; Lipman-Blumen, 1972; Stein, 1971). In fact, Crandall & Battle (1970) found that young women who were highly motivated to achieve in the intellectual sphere also felt that they were able to meet conventional sex-role standards, but had attitudes that were discrepant from those standards in many ways.

Thus, women in general are seen to be having low *n*-Achievement and high *n*-Affiliation but Pathak (1974) has pointed out that girls who go for higher education are most likely to have higher Achievement need.

Brandt (1978) also suggests that movement away from traditional feminine role may be accompanied by a broadening of personality options and integration of both masculine and feminine traits.

Some of the studies do point out that females who are likely to opt for a career are different from those who are planning to be only homemakers (Gysbers & Johnston, 1968).

Garcia (1985) compared women possessing non-traditional careers in selected professional schools of law, medicine, engineering and management with a second sample of women, women enrolled in more traditional graduate programmes of home-economics, nursing, education and library science. Women in non-traditional careers had higher levels of mastery and competitiveness, higher levels of masculine traits, lower levels of feminine traits and higher levels of social competence/self-esteem than women pursuing traditional careers.

Brown (1985) concluded that homemakers and homemaker-graduate women were found to have high affiliation needs and to be committed to home and family. Re-entry women had a more goal directed, intrinsically motivated orientation, characterized by a need for change and excellence in a chosen field.

Hoyt and Kennedy (1958) report that on the EPPS careerists scored higher on Achievement, Intraception, Endurance and lower on Heterosexuality and Succourance. In conclusion Hoyt and Kennedy suggest that career women may be motivated by any of several relatively independent needs and that homemakers are motivated primarily by needs for Affection and Acceptance.

Bledsol (1978) found that women favouring the career role were more radical and imaginative. The young women favouring the homemaker role were more likely to be conservative, excitable, submissive, practical, conscientious and uncontrolled.

Yuen (1980) concluded that career oriented Ss had higher MIQ scores on activity, responsibility and security, while homemakers scored higher on moral values.

The pattern observed among women who are preparing to enter non-traditional career abandoning their stereotyped feminine sex-role identity, is, a large extent, replicated among women who are pursuing non-traditional career.

Even though the number of studies is not very large. Investigators have pointed out that the transition from a traditional homemaker role orientation to Achievement oriented role of a career women has not been brought about without tensions and problems and it has been accompanied by a change in personality pattern of women.

The feminine sex-role stereotype dictates that a woman, regardless of intelligence, education or ability should assume the role of housewife, mother and wife. By assuming this role the college-educated woman forfeits the possibility of direct personal rewards associated with achievement striving but she avoids the negative social consequences of violating sex-role stereotypes. The career woman, on the other hand, is in a position to attain the positive rewards of Achievement striving but must deal with the negative consequences of violating sex-role stereotypes (Burns, 1976).

Biller (1971) has pointed out that women who possess both positive feminine and positive masculine characteristics and secure sex-role orientations are most able to actualize their potentials. Women who have pride in their femininity and are independent and assertive as well as nurturant and sensitive are likely to achieve interpersonal and creative fulfilment.

Burns (1976) found that the measurement profiles for women in different career categories were significantly different from one another. The mean risk taking score for pioneer women was significantly higher than the mean risk taking scores for traditional and no job women. The mean deviance score for pioneer women was significantly higher than those of the traditional and no job women. The mean deviance score for no job women was significantly lower than those of the other two groups. Women whose choices were conventional conformed more closely to stereotyped sex-role behaviour than women in unconventional occupations.

Bachtold and Werner (1972) found women scientists to be serious, radical, confident, dominant, intelligent and adventurous than women in general population and less sociable, group dependent, and sensitive. Personality profiles on the 16 PF of men and women scientists showed strong similarity.

Baruch (1967) and Shelton (1968) in their separate studies found that middle aged professional women had higher Achievement motivation than housewives of comparable ability and economic status.

McKenzie (1972) found that women in conformistic occupation scored significantly lower than those in non-conformistic occupations on dominance, capacity for status, sociability, tolerance, achievement *via* independence, intellectual efficiency and flexibility. Robinson, Perrcta and Brune (1982) concluded that a woman in combining a career and family is not a guaranteed indicator that she is highly autonomous.

Agrawal and Upadhyay (1983) found that females show unconscious dependency needs, show more tendency to "accept and cling to objects" and are more imaginative in their inner life than the males. Females are generally found to be more expressive when they are amid their own sex-group than the males, and this makes them more affiliative.

In the literature reviewed, studies related to single women were hardly to be found. The following two studies have included single women also as one of the comparison groups.

Matter (1982) concluded that single women were younger and better educated, but reported fewers honours and had lower Achievement scores than married women.

Erdwins and Mellinger (1984) compared women in home makers, married/career, single/career and re-entry student roles.

The homemakers obtained highest mean scores on scales designated as responsibility (dependability, conscientiousness) and need to affiliate whereas married/career and single/career women had equivalent means but significantly lower than homemakers. The married/career women scored lowest on self acceptance, need for autonomy and achievement *via* Independence. Homemakers and married/career women do emerge as higher on socialization scale. The authors conclude that significant variation does occur among women who have assumed different life roles. However, on the basis of the study it cannot be ascertained whether these difference emerged after the women undertook these roles or whether personality differences existed as predisposing factor in life role choices.

Review of Studies related to Self-Esteem

Self-concept, the core concept of self-esteem has been a central concept within symbolic interactionism since the seminal writings of Mead (1934), Cooley (1902) and James (1890). But in the past few decades there has been a revitalization of interest in the self-concept specially within social psychology and has acquired a central position in theoretical frameworks and researches.

Numerous dimensions of self-concept have been considered in social psychology but the most elementary distinction is between the content of self-conception (*e.g.* identities) and self-evaluation or in other words self-esteem.

Self-evaluation or self-esteem refers to the evaluative and affective aspects of the self-concept (Wells and Marwell, 1976; Shibutani, 1961). Most researches on the self-concept focus on self-esteem dimension.

Self-esteem is considered to be strongly associated with a sense of competency, power or efficacy, hence a greater attention has been given to this aspect in research on women in employment.

Employment offers a person with greater opportunity to feel a sense of competency, efficiency and greater power over one's own circumstances. Researches support the view that employment can have a positive effect on the self-esteem.

Powers and Sanchez (1982) found that self-esteem was positively correlated with occupation and reading achievement.

Borgatta and Evans (1967), Crowther and More (1972) and Suchner and More (1976) for example found a consistent relationship between occupational prestige and perceptions of such traits as responsibility, competence and intelligence.

But questions concerning the relationship between self-esteem and achievement levels have only recently become important in psychological research. White (1970) discussed the special problems of identity and self-esteem faced by women in science and concluded that interaction with fellow professionals led to heightened self-esteem among them.

In general, however, women are expected to primarily remain involved in housework and household activities. In the initial phases care of children and bringing them up may prove rewarding and result in heightened self-esteem.

Rossi's (1964) data indicate that traditionally socialized young women indeed do fare well during these busy years of early motherhood. At this point in their lives, the family oriented woman has high self-esteem and generally feels good about herself. In sharp contrast, the statistically more deviant, personal achievement-oriented young woman is far more troubled with self-doubt and has low self-esteem during her twenties and early thirties.

However, with growing pattern for smaller families, women hardly are left with any useful activities apart from drudgery of the daily work routine. Commenting upon this phase Rossi (1968) warns us that we must face the alarming possibility that most women lose ground in personal development and self-esteem during the middle years of adulthood whereas most men gain ground. Women maintaining a high level of self-esteem depends on the adequacy of earlier preparation for a shift to, or perhaps more ideally, continuing involvement in major adult roles other than or in addition to marriage and maternity.

Thus, women who have not geared themselves for any other role than homemaker may suffer from what is termed as "Housewife Syndrome". A number of studies report that being merely a housewife may have negative psychological consequences.

Walker and Walker (1980) found that women not employed outside their homes have slightly higher level of anxiety than the employed group.

Holahan and Gilbert (1979) found contrary to prediction, greater role conflict was reported by the non-career group than the career group.

Welch and Booth (1977), Marecek *et al.* (1981) concluded that despite their insulation form job related stresses housewives seem to have either similar or higher levels of psychological and psychosomatic symptoms.

Gove and Tudor (1973) also suggest that a decline in the prestige and skills required in homemaking have led to greater dissatisfaction with homemaking and it has been linked to a higher probability of mental health problems among housewives.

Von der Velden (1974) suggests "decompensations" in the role of housewife as causal, while Bernard (1972) concludes flatly that being a housewife will make a healthy woman sick. Various types of well known problems with the role have been listed by numerous researchers (Bernard, 1972; Oakley, 1974a and 1974b).

Employed women have been found to have better emotional health than housewives in terms of both psychiatric and psychosomatic symptoms. Bart (1970), in a small, non-random sample, found less depression in middle class working women, while fewer psychiatric symptoms were found by Feld (1970), Shaver and Freedman (1976) found lower anxiety, loneliness and feelings of worthlessness among employed women.

Employed women have responded more favourably than housewives on physical and mental health items in a variety of studies. Feld (1963) found that, in a national probability sample of adult women, employed women reported fewer physical health problems and fewer major illness than housewives.

Personal self-esteem has generally been found higher among employed women (Feld, 1963; Hacker, 1971) although feelings of self-esteem do not generalize to confidence regarding motherhood among the employed (Nye, 1974; Sharp, 1963).

Keith and Schafer (1982) concluded that non-traditional sex-role orientations, spending more time at work, receiving help from others and higher self-esteem were linked to less depression.

De Man and Benoit (1982) found that feminists and males reported higher levels of self-esteem than non-feminists. No differences was found between feminists and males. The highest index of relationship was obtained when feminism was correlated simultaneously with self-esteem, age and years of education.

Birnbaum (1971) found that working professional women, whether married or single, by the middle adult years hold themselves in higher regard than equally gifted non-employed women. The professional woman, on the other hand, whether married or single, finds a vital source of personal identity and satisfaction in her work, which greatly enhances her general sense of self-worth.

Mackie (1983) hypothesized that there would be no male-female differences in self-esteem but that full time housewives would have lower self-esteem than women in labour force. Result supports the hypotheses. No sex-differences were found in greater salience or self-esteem. The self-esteem of working wives was significantly higher than that of housewives. However, the family retained its priority for both categories of women.

Evidences, however, are there to show that a large number of housewives maybe perfectly satisfied within their homemaker role and may have self-esteem equal to or higher than employed women. Joshi, Garon and Lechasseur (1984) found no significant differences in self-esteem and loneliness of 40 unemployed women and 40 working women. A negative correlation was obtained between loneliness and self-esteem for both groups.

Erdwins and Mellinger (1984) did not find any differences between married career women, single career women and homemakers on self-esteem.

Keith and Schafer (1980) found that full time homemakers and employed women did not differ in levels of depression. Results of a study by Phadke and Kulkarni (1977) shows that the "employed" and "not-employed" housewives, irrespective of whether they are field-independents or field-dependents do not differ in their adjustment.

Bernard (1972) suggested that those with primary identity as wives and mothers would be sufferers, quite the opposite seems to be true. Marriage, more children and higher education all were associated with being satisfied as housewife. Donelson and Gullahorn's (1977) suggestion that those lacking a strong sense of personal identity would suffer from the syndrome seems more consistent with the findings.

Fidell (1976) concluded that housewife syndrome would appear to be a real phenomenon, but perhaps misleadingly labelled. Because approximately two-thirds of the housewives were as healthy and satisfied as employed women, it is difficult to argue that adopting the role of housewife will make a woman sick. For those with conservative notions about the proper role of women, housewifery would appear to give as much satisfaction as employment does for women with different attitudes. A dissatisfied pattern of responses among housewives, by this analysis would not result from the role itself, but rather from the characteristics of persons who found the role of housewife easier than employment.

The review of the study on self-esteem suggests that it is not sufficient to compare and contrast employed and unemployed women on the self-esteem aspect. It is also essential to look into other personality facets which may effect the self-esteem of the women within various roles.

Hypotheses

Taking into consideration the theoretical basis and the literature reviewed a number of hypotheses have been formulated.

The Married Employed and the Single Employed are expected to be similar and both the groups are expected to be different from married unemployed women on work related needs. On the other hand, both the married groups are expected to be similar to each other but different from single employed women on needs related to homemaker role. The hypotheses related to need variables have been formulated accordingly.

1. Married Employed and Single Employed women are likely to score higher on *n*-Achievement as compared to Married Unemployed Women.
2. Married Employed and Single Employed Women are likely to score lower on *n*-Deference as compared to Married Unemployed Women.
3. Married Employed and Married Unemployed Women are likely to score higher on *n*-Order as compared to Single Employed Women.
4. Married Employed and Single Employed Women are

likely to score higher on *n*-Exhibition as compared to Married Unemployed Women.

5. Married Employed and Single Employed Women are likely to score higher on *n*-Autonomy as compared to Married Unemployed Women.
6. Married Employed and Married Unemployed Women are likely to score higher on *n*-Affiliation as compared to Single Employed Women.
7. Married Employed and Married Unemployed Women are likely to score higher on *n*-Intraception as compared to Single Employed Women.
8. Married Employed and Single Employed Women are likely to score lower on *n*-Succourance as compared to Married Unemployed Women.
9. Married Employed and Single Employed Women are likely to score higher on *n*-Dominance as compared to Married Unemployed Women.
10. Married Employed and Single Employed Women are likely to score lower on *n*-Abasement as compared to Married Unemployed Women.
11. Married Employed and Married Unemployed Women are likely to score higher on *n*-Nurturance as compared to Single Employed Women.
12. Married Employed and Single Employed Women are likely to score higher on *n*-Change as compared to Married Unemployed Women.
13. Married Employed and Single Employed Women are likely to score higher on *n*-Endurance as compared to Married Unemployed Women.
14. Married Employed and Married Unemployed Women are likely to score higher on *n*-Heterosexuality as compared to Single Employed Women.
15. Married Employed and Single Employed Women are likely to score higher on *n*-Aggression as compared to Married Unemployed Women.
16. Married Employed and Single Employed Women are likely to have higher self-esteem than Married Unemployed Women.

3

Research Design and Methodology

Research design is the plan, structure, and strategy of investigation conceived so as to obtain answers to research questions and to control variance. It enables the researcher to answer research questions as validly, objectively, accurately and economically as possible.

In any scientific investigation methodology plays an important role because the reliability and validity of the obtained results are contingent upon the accurate, precise and scientific methodology.

However it does not mean that problems or questions to be asked have to be delimited by the research tool or design available. New innovation are at times required to suit the new requirements of a new problem.

Even though, several standard methodological approaches and designs have been developed and discussed by several authors (Ferguson, 1981; Andrew, 1976), but the choice of the appropriate approach and design ultimately depends on the special characteristics and availability of the sample, nature of measuring instruments and the constraints on the manipulability of invalued variables.

The present investigation is a kind of field study. The main aim of the study was to compare the personality characteristics of women falling into three groups—married employed, married unemployed and single employed. To meet this objectives the research setting within the framework of Field study was considered to be most suitable.

Field studies are *ex-post facto* scientific inquiries aimed at discovering the relations and interactions among sociological, psychological and educational variables in real social structures (Kerlinger, 1964). The studies that are done in life situations like communities, schools, organizations and institutions and that systematically pursue relations and test hypotheses are considered to be field studies (Festinger and Katz, 1953).

Sample

A sample is that part of the universe which we select for the purpose of investigation. A sample should exhibit the characteristics of the universe, it should be a "microcosm," a word which literally means "small universe" (Simpson and Kafka, 1971). There is no fixed opinion about the size of the sample. According to Fisher (1950), large sample is to be preferred than a smaller one. Actually, the sample size is usually determined by the kind of problem to be investigated and the tools used.

The main aim of the present study was to assess the need-patterns and self-esteem of married employed women, married unemployed women and single employed women.

Employed women were defined as those women who were employed full time. The unemployed group consisted of women who are educated but are not employed and are basically housewives.

In order to control the variance which may be caused by taking women from varied professions, employed group consisted of women who were teaching full time in universities only. The housewives were chosen from similar socio-cultural atmosphere, mostly wives of male teaching staff at university.

Lists of the university teachers from some universities (Kashi Vidyapith and Banaras Hindu University) of Varanasi helped to large extent to select the sample. Housewives were approached through personal contact. The subject, thus, selected for the present study were 150 university and college teachers and 75 housewives.

The three groups were chosen in such a way that they matched in age, sex, socio-economic status and educational level. All subjects were residents of Varanasi. The distribution of the final sample is given in Table 3.1.

Table 3.1 : Sample distribution

Group	Age range	Number of subjects
Group I (Married Employed Women)	30-56	75
Group II (Married Unemployed Women)	30-56	75
Group III (Single Employed Women)	30-52	75
Total		225

Considerable time had to be spent in establishing rapport with the subjects and in administering the tests individually, which would have been difficult to accomplish on a larger sample.

Tools

The success of a research investigation to a large extent depends on the choice of appropriate tools which depends on certain factors. It is essential that the tool itself be well standardized, reliable and valid. Secondly, they should be suitable for the sample chosen for the study.

Following self-report measures were used.

Interview Schedule

A semi-structured Interview Schedule has been prepared by the researcher to gain information about the socio-economic background and other social factors like (a) Parental influences. (b) Role of family, (c) Attitude towards career, (d) Home *vs*. Job conflict, (e) Views regarding job related aspects.

The Rosenberg Self-Esteem Questionnaire

To measure self-esteem, Indian Adaptation of Rosenberg Self-

Esteem Questionnaire was used. (Similar to the original version of the scale, Rosenberg, 1965). The scale consists of ten items. Half of the items are positively worded and half of them are negatively worded. The positive and negative items are presented in random order to reduce the effect of respondent set. The items are scored on a four-point scale from strongly agree to strongly disagree. All items are only related to the self-acceptance aspect of self-esteem and not with any other.

The scale is based on Guttman scaling procedure. It considers the unidimensional construct of self-esteem. The scale is brief and through in measuring the self-acceptance factor of self-esteem. It has high reliability for such as short scale and can be used without grouping of items necessary for the Guttman format.

Rosenberg (1965) reported 0.92 reproducibility coefficient for his scale. Silber and Tippett (1965) found a test-retest correlation over two weeks of 0.85 ($N = 28$). Rosenberg (1965) found that this measure correlated with depression and shyness scale. The person with high self-esteem shows more assertiveness and more extra-curricular activities and less shyness and depression.

The Rosenberg Self-Esteem Questionnaire has been adapted for Indian population (Prashant, 1988) taking into consideration the basic technical requirements. All items were translated into Hindi. Back translation was done by bilinguals and was found to be similar to the original set of items. The Hindi version was then administered on an Indian sample ($N = 100$). The coefficient of reproducibility was checked for the Indian version and was found to be 0.89.

High score on the test indicates low self-esteem, coefficient of test-retest reliability was found to be 0.80. Validity was checked by correlating the test with Beck Depression Inventory and it was found to be 0.45.

Tripathi Personal Preference Schedule

This schedule is a multitrait scale of 15 normal personality variables (Tripathi, 1973). These variables are originally based on the list of manifest needs described by Murray (1938). A special feature of the schedule is that the social desirability variable has been controlled by the use of forced choice format of items. The respondent is expected to choose one item out of a pair of items. 210 such pairs of items are given in the schedule. The items of each pair are selected in such a way that they are nearest on the social desirability scale value.

The statements were derived basically from Edwards Personal Preference schedule but the pairings are not similar since social desirability values vary with culture. For development and standardization college sample has been used. The need variables which have been covered are presented below along with a brief description of the same.

(i) *Achievement (Ach)* : To do one's best, to be successful, to accomplish tasks requiring skill and effort, to be a recognized authority, to accomplish something of great significance, to do a difficult job well, to solve difficult problems and puzzles, to be able to do things better than others, to write a great novel or play.

(ii) *Deference (Def)* : To get suggestions from others, to find out what others think, to follow instructions and do what is expected, to praise others, to tell others that they have done a good job, to accept the leadership of others, to read about great men, to conform to custom and avoid the unconventional, to let others make decision.

(iii) *Order (Ord)* : To have written work neat and organized, to make plans before starting on a difficult task, to have things organized, to keep things neat and orderly, to make advance plans when taking a trip, to organize details of work, to keep letters and files according to some system, to have meals organized and a definite time for eating, to make things arranged so that they run smoothly without change.

(iv) *Exhibition (Exh)* : To say witty and clever things, to tell amusing jokes and stories, to talk about personal adventures and experiences, to have others notice and comment upon one's appearance, to say things just to see what effect it will have on others, to talk about personal achievements, to be the centre of attention, to use words that others do not know the meaning of, to ask questions others cannot answer.

(v) *Autonomy (Aut)* : To be able to come and go as desired, to say what one thinks about things, to be independent of others in making decisions, to feel free to do what one wants, to do things that are unconventional, to avoid situations where one is expected to conform, to do things without regard to what others may think, to criticize those in positions of authority, to avoid responsibilities and obligations.

(vi) *Affiliation (Aff)* : To be loyal to friends, to participate in friendly groups, to do things for friends, to form new friendships, to make as many friends as possible, to share things with friends, to do things with friends rather than alone, to form strong attachments, to write letters to friends.

(vii) *Intraception (Int)* : To analyze one's motives and feelings, to observe others, to understand how others feel about problems, to put one's self in another's place, to judge people by why they do things rather than by what they do , to analyze the behaviour of others, to analyze the motives of others, to predict how others will act.

(viii) *Succourance (Suc)* : To have others provide help when in trouble, to seek encouragement from others, to have others be kindly, to have others be sympathetic and understanding about personal problems, to receive a great deal of affection from others, to have others do favours cheerfully, to be helped by others when depressed, to have others feel sorry when one is sick, to have a fuss made over one when hurt.

(ix) *Dominance (Dom)* : To argue for one's point of view, to be a leader in groups to which one belongs, to be regarded by others as a leader, to be elected or appointed Chairman of Committees to make group decisions, to settle arguments and disputes between others, to persuade and influence others, to do what one wants, to supervise and direct the actions of others, to tell others how to do their jobs.

(x) *Abasement (Aba)* : To feel guilty when one does something wrong, to accept blame when things do not go right, to feel that personal pain and misery suffered does more good than harm, to feel the need for punishment for wrong doing, to feel better when giving in and avoiding a fight than when having one's own way, to feel the need for confession of errors, to feel depressed by inability to handle situations, to feel timid in the presence of superiors, to feel inferior to others in most respects.

(xi) *Nurturance (Nur)* : To help friends when they are in trouble, to assist others less fortunate, to treat others with kindness, and sympathy, to forgive others, to do small favours for others to be generous with others, to sympathize with others, who are hurt or sick, to show a great deal of affection toward others, to have others confide in one about personal problems.

(xii) *Change (Chg)* : To do new and different things, to travel, to meet new people, to experience novelty and change in daily routine, to experiment and try new things, to eat in new and different places, to try new and different jobs, to move about the country and live in different places.

(xiii) *Endurance (End)* : To keep at a job until it is finished, to complete any job undertaken, to work hard at a task, to keep at a puzzle or problem until it is solved, to work at a single job before taking on others, to stay up late working in order to get a job done, to put in long hours of work without distraction, to stick at a problem even though it may seem as if no progress is being made, to avoid being interrupted while at work.

(xiv) *heterosexuality (Het)* : To go out with members of the opposite sex, to engage in social activities with the opposite sex, to make friends with opposite sex, to be regarded as physically attractive by those of opposite sex, to participate in discussions about sex, to read books and plays involving sex, to listen to or tell jokes involving sex, to engage oneself in conversation with those of opposite sex.

(xv) *Aggression (Agg)* : To attack contrary points of view, to tell others what one thinks about them, to criticize others publicly, to make fun of others, to tell others off when disagreeing with them, to get revenge for insults, to become angry, to blame others when things go wrong, to read newspaper accounts of violence.

Reliability : The internal consistency of each of the sub-scale has been found to be quite satisfactory since the split half coefficient of correlations between scores of rows and those on columns ranges from 0.82 to 0.99. Regarding the consistency also it was revealed that the lowest coefficient of correlation is 0.66 to 0.74.

Validity : The convergent validity as assessed through correlation of TPPS scores and TAT was found to be quite high (0.56 to 0.93). The discriminant validity was investigated by correlating the scores on Sinha Anxiety Scale. The correlations were found to be quite low ranging from 0.00 to 0.24.

Scoring : First the scoring for consistency scores is done using a scoring template. The diagonal slit in the template cut across the consistency items which are not to be counted in obtaining scores for personality variables. Consistency score is counted on the basis of tallying—the responses given to items on the diagonal and their duplicate items which can be seen through the other slits on the template.

Now the scores for need variables are counted both row-wise and column-wise. All '*Kas*' in the first row and all '*Khas*' in the first column represent items for *n*-Achievement. Similarly all '*Kas*' in succeeding rows and all '*Khas*' in their respective columns represent the corresponding need variables. The row and column totals added together give the score for each need variable.

Method of Data Collection

The data collection was done individually. The Interview Schedule was given first followed by TPPS and self-esteem scale. However, later it was observed that subjects would often leave the TPPS midway due to its length, hence, in later administration TPPS was presented first followed by interview schedule and self-esteem questionnaire.

Employed women whether single or married use to finish the administration session in one sitting but married unemployed use to take two or three sitting due to disturbances or boredom.

Statistics Applied

After the data collection all the tests were scored according to the respective manuals and instructions. The scores thus obtained were further subjected to statistical treatment. Mean and SD were calculated for each group on each dimension separately. One way ANOVA (Ferguson, 1971) was performed on the scores and '*t*' tests were applied to ascertain whether intergroup differences exist or not.

Furthermore the groups were also divided into high scorers and low scorers on the basis of *n*-Achievement and Self-esteem scores Inter- and Intra-group comparisons were made.

Subjects having High Scores on *n*-Achievement were compared with low scorers within each group and Inter-group differences were also estimated using '*t*' test for high and low scorers.

'*t*' test was also used to ascertain similar intra- and inter-group differences for high and low self-esteem subjects.

Data from Interview Schedule was classified into categories and Chi-square test was applied to it.

The results thus obtained were organized and present in tabular form for analysis.

4

Results, Analysis and Discussion

Intergroup Differences on Need Variables

The Mean and SD on need scores for the three comparison groups, Married Employed (ME), Married Unemployed (MUE), and Single Employed (SE), women have been presented in Tables 4.1, 4.4, 4.7, 4.10, 4.13, 4.16, 4.19, 4.22, 4.25, 4.28, 4.31, 4.34, 4.37, 4.40 and 4.43.

The *F* ratios computed on the basis of one way ANOVA for the various needs have been presented in Tables 4.2, 4.5, 4.8, 4.11, 4.14, 4.17, 4.20, 4.23, 4.26, 4.29, 4.32, 4.35, 4.38, 4.41 and 4.44.

t test was applied to compare the means for each pair of groups. The results have been given in Tables 4.3, 4.6, 4.9, 4.12, 4.15, 4.18, 4.21, 4.24, 4.27, 4.30, 4.33, 4.36, 4.39, 4.42 and 4.45.

Need for Achievement

One way ANOVA on need for Achievement at scores revealed an *F* ratio of 27.508 (Table 4.2), the value is significant at 0.01 level. This indicates that intergroup differences exist on *n*-Ach. A look at the Means (Table 4.1) and '*t*' values (Table 4.3) clearly indicates that ME (M 15.30) and SE (M 15.49) have equally high scores on *n*-Ach and the difference is statistically not significant. However, both these groups significantly differ from MUE (M 13.27).

It is apparent from the results that the employed women have higher n-Ach as compared to unemployed women irrespective of their marital status.

Table 4.1 : Mean and S. D. of *n*-Achievement Scores for Married Employed (ME), Married Unemployed (MUE), and Single Employed (SE) groups

	ME	MUE	SE
Mean	15.30	13.27	15.49
S. D.	3.523	3.83	8.406
N	75	75	75

Table 4.2 : Summary table for one way ANOVA on *n*-Achievement Scores

Source of Variation	Sum of squares	df	Variance	*F*	*p*
Between	644.916	2	322.45778		
Within	2602.40	222	11.72252	27.508	.01
Total	3247.32	224	14.49694		

Table 4.3 : '*t*'-values indicating intergroup differences on *n*-Achievement Scores

	ME *vs.* MUE	MUE *vs.* SE	ME *vs.* SE
t	3.38	2.08	0.18
p	0.01	0.05	N.S.

ME = Married Employed; MUE = Married Unemployed; SE = Single Employed
N.S. —Not Significant

The results confirm the Hypothesis No. 1 which states that Married Employed and Single Employed women are likely to score higher on *n*-Achievement as compared to Married Unemployed Women.

n-Ach. refers to the need to be successful, to do one's best, to accomplish tasks requiring skill and effort, to be recognized as authority, to accomplish something of great significance, to work on difficult problems, jobs etc.

This high *n*-Achievement may probably be the reason why the employed women have chosen to compete and enter a work field where they may be able to realise their potentials and need to excel in chosen fields.

The unemployed women also came from a group which was educated and could possibly have taken up employment if they chose to, but the fact that they did not, may be due to their lower need for achievement.

Baruch (1967) and Shelton (1968) had found that middle aged professional women had higher achievement motivation than housewives of comparable ability and economic status.

When women in conformistic and non-conformisitc professions were compared by McKenzie (1972) it was found that the former were lower on Achievement via Independence.

Brown (1985) had also found that re-entry women *i.e.* women entering graduation courses again after a gap due to marriage, had greater need for excellence in a chosen field *i.e.* Achievement striving as compared to homemakers.

Hoyt and Kennedy (1958) had found that careerists scored higher on *n*-Achievement.

Need for Deference

On need for Deference the Mean scores of the three groups ME, MUE and SE are not too different from each other (Table 4.4). In one way ANOVA (Table 4.5) also the *F* ratio has not been found to be significant and none of the '*t*' values are significant (Table 4.6).

n-Deference reflects characteristics like following instructions, doing what is expected, accepting leadership of others, avoiding unconventional, conforming to customs, praising others and let others take decisions.

Table 4.4: Mean and S. D. of *n*-Deference scores for Married Employed (ME), Married Unemployed (MUE), and Single Employed (SE) groups

	ME	MUE	SE
Mean	13.35	12.64	13.46
S. D	2.8089	2.6514	3.7389
N	75	75	75

Table 4.5: Summary table for one way ANOVA on *n*-Deference Scores

Source of Variation	Sum of squares	*df*	Variance	*F*	*p*
Between	29.3067	2	14.65333		
Within	2188.85	222	9.85970	1.486	N.S.
Total	2218.16	224	9.90250		

Table 4.6 : '*t*'-values indicating intergroup differences on *n*-Deference Scores

	ME *vs.* MUE	MUE *vs.* SE	ME *vs.* SE
t	1.59	1.55	0.20
p	N.S.	N.S.	N.S.

The results indicate no differences between the three groups on *n*-Def. Thus it can be said that women whether they are employed or unemployed, single or married, are equally Deferent in their personality structure.

The results do not confirm the Hypothesis No. 2 which stated that Married Employed and Single Employed Women are likely to score lower on *n*-Deference as compared to Married Unemployed Women.

The results are also not in consonance with those of Bledsol (1978) who found that women favouring the homemaker role were more submissive than those favouring career role.

In fact taking into account the Indian social mileu in which these women have been brought up they would have been taught, to be obedient, irrespective of the fact that they may be given freedom to move out and may be capable of taking decision and acting on their own.

Need for Order

On need for Order also the Mean scores are almost equal for the three groups (Table 4.7). Even though the ME have the lowest score. The *F* ratio (Table 4.8) is not significant and nor are the '*t*' values (Table 4.9).

All the three groups appear to be equally high, on *n*-Ord as the differences are not significant.

Table 4. 7: Mean and S.D. of *n*-Order Scores for Married Employed (ME), Married Unemployed (MUE), and Single Employed (SE) groups

	ME	MUE	SE
Mean	14.58	15.14	15.19
S. D.	3.528	3.265	3.408
N	75	75	75

Table 4.8 : Summary table for one way ANOVA on *n*-Order Scores

Source of Variation	Sum of Squares	*df*	Variance	*F*	*p*
Between	17.3156	2	8.65778		
Within	2634.40	222	11.86667	0.730	N.S.
Total	2651.72	224	11.83802		

Table 4.9 : '*t*' values indicating intergroup differences on *n*-Order Scores

	ME *vs.*MUE	MUE *vs.* SE	ME *vs.* SE
t	1.01	0.10	1.08
p	N.S.	N.S.	N.S.

Hypothesis No. 3 which stated that Married Employed and Married Unemployed Women are likely to score higher on *n*-Order as compared to Single Employed Women stands rejected.

n-Order connotes characteristics like being organized, keeping things in a neat and orderly manner, being systematic, having set timings for specific work and planning everything carefully.

All women are trained and prepared to manage a household and all these characteristics appear to be related to this aspect of training. When subjects were asked to report what their parents had planned for their future (Table 4.72). Most of them did report that either marriage alone or marriage along with career was planned for them. A very small number reported that only career was planned by their parents under these circumstances it is to be expected that all women irrespective of whether they eventually take a career or not will be trained by their parents to handle their household well.

Need for Exhibition

On need for Exhibition the *F* ratio has been found to be 6.677 and the value is significant at 0.01 level (Table 4.11). It is indicated that the groups differ on need for exhibition. A view of the Tables 4.10 and 4.12 shows that MUE have the highest score (M 12.58) on need exhibition whereas difference in mean scores of ME (M 11.06) and SE (M 11.60) is not significant. Differences between scores of ME *vs.* MUE and MUE *vs.* SE are statistically significantly at 0.01 and 0.05 levels.

Table 4.10: Mean and S. D. of *n*-Exhibition Scores for Married Employed (ME), Married Unemployed (MUE), and Single Employed (SE) groups

	ME	MUE	SE
Mean	11.06	12.58	11.60
S. D.	2.379	2.703	2.535
N	75	75	75

Table 4.11 : Summary table for one way ANOVA on *n*-Exhibition Scores

Source of Variation	Sum of Squares	*df*	Variance	*F*	*E*
Between	88.9156	2	44.45778		
Within	1478.13	222	6.65826	6.677	0.01
Total	1567.05	224	6.99575		

Table 4.12 : '*t*'-values indicating intergroup differences on *n*-Exhibition Scores

	ME *vs.* MUE	MUE *vs.* SE	ME *vs.* SE
t	3.67	2.30	1.35
p	0.01	0.05	N.S.

Person with high *n*-Exhibition likes to say witty and clever things, to tell amusing jokes and stories, to talk about personal adventures and experiences, wants others to notice and comment upon one's appearance.

On *n*-Exhibition the two employed groups are quite similar and the married unemployed group has a significantly higher score. It can be said that MUE women have a greater need for exhibition than the employed.

The results are contradictory to the Hypothesis No. 4 which states that Married Employed and Single Employed Women are likely to score higher on *n*-Exhibition as compared to Married Unemployed Women.

In fact each person has a desire to be recognised and proclaimed to be interesting and different from others. The employed women channelize these desires into their achievement related fields but the unemployed have no such channel hence, behaviour patterns reflecting exhibitionism may be their way of proclaiming their own importance.

Need for Autonomy

One way ANOVA on need for Autonomy score (Table 4.14) has revealed an *F* ratio of 5.149 ($p < 0.01$). A perusal of Tables 4.13 and 4.15 indicates that the SE women are significantly different from both ME and MUE groups. The latter two groups are similar to each other. Difference between *n*-Autonomy scores of ME and MUE women is not significant but between ME *vs*. SE and MUE *vs*. SE are significant at 0.05 and 0.01 level.

Table 4.13 : Mean and S. D. of *n*-Autonomy Scores for Married Employed (ME), Married Unemployed (MUE), and Single Employed (SE) groups

	ME	MUE	SE
Mean	14.96	14.51	16.19
S. D.	3.386	3.505	2.932
N	75	75	75

Table 4.14 : Summary table for one way ANOVA on *n*-Autonomy Scores

Source of Variation	Sum of Squares	*df*	Variance	*F*	*P*
Between	113.316	2	56.65778		
Within	2443.01	222	11.00456	5.149	0.01
Total	2556.33	224	11.41218		

Table 4.15 : '*t*'-values indicating intergroup differences on *n*-Autonomy Scores

	ME *vs*. MUE	MUE *vs*. SE	ME *vs*. SE
t	0.80	3.18	2.38
p	N.S.	0.01	0.05

The single employed group has the highest score (M 16.19) on *n*-Autonomy and they are significantly different from both the married groups. The married groups ME (M 14.96) and MUE (M 14.51) are similar to each other and have scored lower on *n*-Autonomy.

The results partially support the Hypothesis No. 5 which states that Married Employed and Single Employed Women are likely to score higher on *n*-Autonomy as compared to Married Unemployed Women.

A high *n*-Autonomy would mean that the person would like to be free in his movements, speech and in making decisions. Such a person would avoid situations where one is expected to conform and would not necessarily like to remain under the authority of others. In the Indian socio-cultural set-up, women once married have to curb their desire for free thinking and movement. They are expected to follow and accept the authority of the husband and the in-laws. Even though prior to marriage girls are expected to remain under the authority of the parents but as they become older and take up professions the parents may not be there to exercise their authority either due to living elsewhere or death. In this way employed women may enjoy a sense of complete autonomy especially when they are single and may prefer to remain so if their *n*-Autonomy is very high.

Need for Affiliation

It can be seen from Table 4.16 that the Mean scores for the three comparison groups on *n*-Affiliation are 14.81 (ME), 14.87 (MUE), and 15.10 (SE). The results of one way ANOVA (Table 4.17) and the '*t*' test (Table 4.18) both indicate that the three groups do not differ on *n*-Affiliation. The *F* ratio and all the '*t*' values are not significant. Women irrespective of their marital or employment status appear to have equally strong *n*-Affiliation.

Table 4.16: Mean and S. D. of *n*-Affiliation Scores for Married Employed (ME), Married Unemployed (MUE), and Single Employed (SE) groups

	ME	MUE	SE
Mean	14.813	14.87	15.10
S. D.	4.373	3.088	3.067
N	75	75	75

Hypothesis No. 6 stated that Married Employed and Married Unemployed Women are likely to score higher on *n*-Affiliation as compared to Single Employed Women. But the results do not support this hypothesis.

n-Affiliation indicates a need to be loyal to friends, to share and participate with friends and to form strong attachment. In fact it has been investigated and found in various studies that women in general have a strong affiliation need. Socially they are reared in a manner that they are the care taker of the social and the affiliative responsibilities of the family. The responsibility that the family remain socially and emotionally entact lies on the shoulders of women only.

Table 4.17 : Summary table for one way ANOVA on *n*-Affiliation Scores

Source of Variation	Sum of Squares	*df*	Variance	*F*	*P*
Between	3.31556	2	1.65778		
Within	2436.40	222	10.97477	0.151	N.S.
Total	2439.72	224	10.89159		

Table 4.18 : '*t*'-values indicating intergroup differences on *n*-Affiliation Scores

	ME *vs.* MUE	MUE *vs.* SE	ME *vs.* SE
t	0.10	0.46	0.47
p	N.S.	N.S.	N.S.

Thus, from the earlier ages itself women are encouraged for activities which promote affiliation. In fact it has been argued that women's achievement related activities are also affiliation oriented.

They may desire to do something excellent or important not for the sake of the work itself but for the sake of someone loved or respected by them. Women also have a great need to talk and share their thoughts and this is in consonance with high *n*-Affiliation.

Need for Intraception

The Mean scores on *n*-Intraception are 14.28 for ME, 13.36 for MUE and 13.38 for SE (Table 4.19).

On Tables 4.20 and 4.21 the F ratio and t ratio have been given and it can be seen that none of the values are significant.

Thus the three groups do not differ on *n*-Intraception.

Table 4.19: Mean and S. D. of *n*-Intraception Scores for Married Employed (ME), Married Unemployed (MUE), and Single Employed (SE) groups

	ME	MUE	SE
Mean	14.28	13.36	13.38
S. D.	3.527	3.807	2.851
N	75	75	75

Table 4.20 : Summary table for one way ANOVA on *n*-Intraception Scores

Source of Variation	Sum of Squares	*df*	Variance	*F*	*P*
Between	35.9467	2	17.97333		
Within	2379.41	222	10.71808	1.677	N.S.
Total	2415.36	224	10.78286		

Table 4.21 : '*t*'-values indicating intergroup differences on *n*-Intraception Scores

	ME *vs.* MUE	MUE *vs.* SE	ME *vs.* SE
t	1.53	0.04	1.72
p	N.S.	N.S.	N.S.

The results are not in consonance with Hypothesis No. 7 which states that Married Employed and Married Unemployed Women are likely to score higher on *n*-Intraception as compared to Single Employed Women.

Intraception refers to the need to analyze and understand one's own motives and feelings and that of others and to empathize with others. Since women have a greater *n*-Affiliation they are likely to be equally Intraceptive because the process of affiliation would require a good understanding of another person.

The results indicate women whether married, unmarried, employed or unemployed tend to be equally analytical of their own behaviour and that of the others.

Need for Succourance

On need for succourance MUE women have the highest Mean score of 15.38 and their Mean score differs significantly ($p < .01$) from the Mean scores of both ME (13.23), and SE (13.44) groups.

Differences between Mean scores of ME and SE are not significant. The results confirm the Hypothesis No. 8 which states that Married Employed and Single Employed Women are likely to score lower on *n*-Succourance as compared to Married Unemployed Women.

Table 4.22: Mean and S. D. of *n*-Succourance Scores for Married Employed (ME), Married Unemployed (MUE), and Single Employed (SE) groups

	ME	MUE	SE
Mean	13.23	15.38	13.44
S. D.	3.722	3.633	3.963
N	75	75	75

Table 4.23 : Summary table for one way ANOVA on *n*-Succourance Scores

Source of Variation	Sum of Squares	*df*	Variance	*F*	*p*
Between	34.0356	2	17.01778		
Within	3803.55	222	17.13309	0.993	N.S.
Total	3837.58	224	17.13206		

On succourance thus the MUE group have the highest score and they are significantly different from both the married and single employed women. The ME and SE groups are not different from each other.

High need for succourance denotes a general tendency for dependency. Highly succourant people expect others to be kind, sympathetic, encouraging, understanding, ready to provide help when in trouble. They want others to feel sorry for them and make a fuss when hurt or sick. They seek favour from others and want a great deal of affection from others. These characteristics fit in very well with the conventional image of a woman who is perpetually dependent on others.

Table 4.24 : '*t*'-values indicating intergroup differences on *n*-Succourance Scores

	ME *vs.* MUE	MUE *vs.* SE	ME *vs.* SE
t	3.596	3.12	0.34
p	0.01	0.01	N.S.

The employed women has to move outside and independently. She has to take decisions and perform in relation to her job related responsibilities without seeking the support of others. Under these circumstances it is natural that they should be less succourant.

Table 4.25: Mean and S. D. of *n*-Dominance Scores for Married Employed (ME), Married Unemployed (MUE), and Single Employed (SE) groups

	ME	MUE	SE
Mean	12.46	12.52	14
S.D.	3.054	4.435	3.241
N	75	75	75

Need for Dominance

The Mean scores for the three comparison groups on *n*-Dominance (Table 4.22) are 12.46 (ME), 12.52 (MUE), and 14 (SE). The *F* ratio for one way ANOVA (Table 4.26) is significant at 0.05 level. A look at the Table 4.27 indicates that ME and MUE groups are not significantly different but the SE group differ significantly from both ME and MUE groups.

Table 4.26 : Summary table for one way ANOVA on *n*-Dominance Scores

Source of Variation	Sum of Squares	*df*	Variance	*F*	*p*
Between	114.676	2	57.33778		
Within	2975.31	222	13.40228	4.278	0.05
Total	3089.98	224	13.79456		

Table 4.27: '*t*'-values indicating intergroup differences on *n*-Dominance Scores

	ME *vs.* MUE	MUE *vs.* SE	ME *vs.* SE
t	0.10	2.34	3.00
p	N.S.	0.05	0.01

The single employed women have the highest score on *n*-Dominance and they are significantly different from the two married groups.

The results partially confirm the Hypothesis No. 9 which states that Married Employed and Single Employed Women are likely to score higher on *n*-Dominance as compared to Married Unemployed Women.

A high *n*-Dominance is associated with characteristics like desire to be a leader, to influence, to persuade, to supervise, and direct others. A dominant person considers his own point of view to be most important and tries to impose these on others.

In the Indian socio-cultural context a woman is not expected to be dominant within the family set-up. In fact women who are highly dominant would find it uncomfortable to be in the married role. It has already been found that the single employed women are high on *n*-Autonomy seen in combination it would appear that these single women may have preferred to remain single since the married role would have failed to satisfy some of these predominant needs.

Need for Abasement

The Mean scores on *n*-Abasement are 15.05 (ME), 15.32 (MUE), and 14.40 (SE). However, the *F* ratio is not significant (Table 4.29). The '*t*' values presented in (Table 4.30) show a significant difference between Mean scores of MUE and SE only. Differences between scores of ME *vs*. MUE and ME *vs*. SE are not significant.

Table 4.28: Mean and S. D. of *n*-Abasement Scores for Married Employed (ME), Married Unemployed (MUE), and Single Employed (SE) groups

	ME	MUE	SE
Mean	15.05	15.32	14.40
S. D.	2.86	2.89	2.545
N	75	75	75

Table 4.29 : Summary table for one way ANOVA on *n*-Abasement Scores

Source of Variation	Sum of Squares	*df*	Variance	*F*	*p*
Between	33.6089	2	16.80444		
Within	1730.11	222	7.79327	2.156	N.S.
Total	1763.72	224	7.87373		

Table 4.30 : '*t*'-values indicating intergroup differences on *n*-Abasement Scores

	ME *vs*. MUE	MUE *vs*. SE	ME *vs*. SE
t	0.57	2.07	1.47
p	N.S.	0.05	N.S.

On *n*-Abasement the married unemployed have the highest score, married employed being next, followed by single employed who have the lowest score. However, differences are significant only between MUE and SE group.

Results partially confirm Hypothesis No. 10 which states that Married Employed and Single Employed Women are likely to score lower on *n*-Abasement as compared to Married Unemployed Women.

n-Abasement is characterized by sense of guilt, acceptance of blame, timidity, sense of inferiority, feeling of pain and misery and feeling responsible of any wrong doing. Thus a person having high *n*-Abasement would not be feeling very good about himself. Taking into consideration the results given on (Tables 4.46, 4.47, and 4.48) related to self-esteem. It appears that MUE women who have the lowest self-esteem also have the highest *n*-Abasement. The married women as such finds herself in a position where she is held responsible for any thing that goes wrong in the household. From the earlier age also girls are more strongly inculcated into the culture of taking responsibility for all that goes wrong. In many cases the child may be made to feel guilty due to sheer fact of being born a girl. This earlier training combined with perpetuation of the same practice after the marriage through different agencies like inlaws or husband is likely to lead to a higher *n*-Abasement among married women.

Need for Nurturance

The Mean scores on *n*-Nurturance for the three groups are almost equal as can be seen from Table 4.31. Neither the *F* ratio nor the 't' values (Tables 4.32 & 4.33) are significant.

Hypothesis No. 11 which states that Married Employed and Married Unemployed Women are likely to score higher on *n*-Nurturance as compared to Single Employed Women stands rejected.

Nurturance generally refers to a desire to take care of others. Such persons like to help, assist, show kindness and sympathy or forgiveness. They like to do favours and are generous. They show affection towards others and like others confinding in them. All the three groups are equally high on nurturance.

Table 4.31: Mean and S. D. of *n*-Nurturance Scores for Married Employed (ME), Married Unemployed (MUE), and Single Employed (SE) groups

	ME	MUE	SE
Mean	17.86	18.13	17.80
S. D.	2.707	3.0805	2.699
N	75	75	75

Table 4.32 : Summary table for one way ANOVA on *n*-Nurturance Scores

Source of Variation	Sum of Squares	*df*	Variance	*F*	*p*
Between	4.54222	2	2.27111		
Within	1838.59	222	8.28192	0.274	N.S.
Total	1843.13	224	8.22825		

Table 4.33 : '*t*'-values indicating intergroup differences on *n*-Nurturance Scores

	ME *vs.* MUE	MUE *vs.* SE	ME *vs.* SE
t	0.57	0.70	0.14
p	N.S.	N.S.	N.S.

The Indian socio-cultural set-up promotes development of the nurturant characteristics in women. They are promoted to be kind, sympathetic and caring towards others. Observation of games of small children would also show that most of the young girl prefer to play with dolls treating the dolls as small dependent. Children are taking care of them. Their games reflect the role for which they are preparing themselves. In fact this very nurturant trait at times goes against the competitiveness required for achievement orientation.

Need for Change

Mean scores of the three comparison groups on *n*-change (Table 4.34) are 15.306 (ME), 16.413 (MUE), and 13.746 (SE). The *F* ratio of 9.824 is significant at 0.01 level (Table 4.35). The '*t*' value for difference between ME *vs.* MUE groups is not significant but for ME *vs.* SE groups '*t*' is significant at 0.05 level and for MUE *vs.* SE it is significant at 0.01 level.

On need for change both the married groups are significantly higher than the single employed group.

Table 4.34: Mean and S. D. of *n*-Change Scores for Married Employed (ME), Married Unemployed (MUE), and Single Employed (SE) groups

	ME	MUE	SE
Mean	15.306	16.413	13.746
S. D.	4.643	2.88	4.67
N	75	75	75

Table 4.35 : Summary table for one way ANOVA on *n*-Change Scores

Source of Variation	Sum of Squares	*df*	Variance	*F*	*p*
Between	230.507	2	115.25333		
Within	2604.45	222	11.73177	9.824	0.01
Total	2834.96	224	12.65607		

Table 4.36 : *t*-values indicating intergroup differences on *n*-Change Scores

	ME *vs.* MUE	MUE *vs.* SE	ME *vs.* SE
t	1.74	4.20	2.05
p	N.S.	0.01	0.05

Results do not support Hypothesis No. 12 which states that Married Employed and Single Employed Women are likely to score higher on *n*-Change as compared to Married Unemployed Women.

The need for change is reflected in the desire to do new things, travel to meet new people, try out new facts and fashion, eat new and different things. It would appear that the single women would prefer that the things remain as they are and they would not necessarily appreciate a lot of change in their life style. This would reflect a certain amount of regidity in contrast to liability expected from a woman in a married role.

A married woman would need to adjust to various changes and variations caused within the households due to lifestyles of different members of the family. Whenever a single woman can lead the life according to whatever pattern she may set for herself which is in consonance with a lower need for change.

Need for Endurance

On *n*-Endurance the Mean scores are 16.826 for ME, 16.04 for

MUE and 17.346 for SE groups (Table 4.37). The *F* ratio for one way ANOVA is significant at 0.05 level (Table 4.38). However, differences between ME *vs*. MUE and ME *vs*. SE have not been found to be significant. Only difference between MUE *vs*. SE are significant at 0.05 level.

Table 4.37 : Mean and S. D. of *n*-Endurance Scores for Married Employed (ME), Married Unemployed (MUE), and Single Employed (SE) groups

	ME	MUE	SE
Mean	16.826	16.04	17.346
S.D.	6.598	3.627	3.49
N	75	75	75

Table 4.38 : Summary table for one way ANOVA on *n*-Endurance Scores

Source of Variation	Sum of Squares	*df*	Variance	*F*	*p*
Between	96.0267	2	48.01333		
Within	3504.61	222	15.78655	3.041	0.05
Total	3600.64	224	16.07429		

Table 4.39 : *t*-values indicating intergroup differences on *n*-Endurance Scores

	ME *vs*. MUE	MUE *vs*. SE	ME *vs*. SE
t	0.91	2.25	0.604
p	N.S.	0.05	N.S.

Hypothesis No. 13 is only partially confirmed. It states that Married Employed and Single Employed Women are likely to score higher on *n*-Endurance as compared to Married Unemployed Women.

On Endurance the SE has the highest score but only the difference between single employed women and married unemployed women is significant. People with high *n*-Endurance generally work very hard, put in long hours, stick at a problem, avoid being interrupted and like to finish whatever they start. They do not like to leave any work half done.

The SE appears to be highest on this trait and the MUE the lowest. The ME group lies in the middle but it neither differs significantly from MUE or SE groups. The married women, thus, do not appear to be as enduring as the single women. Possibly the fact that single women do not have to make adjustments with the demand of others as much as the married women has to an important role to play in context to endurance. It is probable that basically these women do not differ but the demands of the married role may reduce their *n*-Endurance.

Need for Heterosexuality

On *n*-Heterosexuality the *F* ratio for one way ANOVA was found to be 13.587 ($p<0.01$) as presented in Table 4.41. This indicates that the three groups are likely to be different from each other. All the '*t*' values presented in Table 4.42 are significant. It can be observed from Table 4.40 that MUE have the highest Mean score (8.746) followed by ME (7.44) and SE have the lowest Mean score (6.346).

Table 4.40: Mean and S. D. of *n*-Heterosexuality Scores for Married Employed (ME), Married Unemployed (MUE), and Single Employed (SE) groups

	ME	MUE	SE
Mean	7.44	8.746	6.346
S. D.	3.304	2.648	2.366
N	75	75	75

Table 4.41 : Summary table for one way ANOVA on *n*-Heterosexuality Scores

Source of Variation	Sum of Squares	*df*	Variance	*F*	*p*
Between	245.982	2	122.99111		
Within	2009.57	222	9.05213	13.587	0.01
Total	2255.56	224	10.06944		

Table 4.42: *t*-values indicating intergroup differences on *n*-Heterosexuality Scores

	ME *vs.* MUE	MUE *vs.* SE	ME *vs.* SE
t	2.68	5.85	2.28
p	0.01	0.01	0.05

Results confirm the Hypothesis No. 14 which states that Married Employed and Married Unemployed Women are likely to score higher on *n*-Heterosexuality as compared to Single Employed Women.

The results indicate that the MUE group has the highest scores on *n*-Heterosexuality and the single employed have the lowest. The Married Employed fall in the middle of the two groups.

Heterosexuality refers to the need to associate with members of opposite sex, to be regarded as physically attractive, to read about and discuss sex and to take interest in the member of opposite sex.

It is understandable that MUE who are in the housewife role and the housewifery duties are primary for them hence, their higher level of heterosexuality is compatible with their present role. The low score of single employed is also meaningful since they are in a role which does not permit opportunities for the fulfilment of this need.

The married employed who play the dual role of housewife and outside worker appear to have a level of need heterosexuality which strikes a balance between the two roles.

Need for Aggression

On *n*-Aggression the Mean scores for ME group is 11.56, for MUE group it is 11.88 and for SE women the mean score is 10.28. On Table 4.44 results of one way ANOVA on need Aggression scores indicates that *F* ratio is significant at 0.01 level.

The results of the '*t*' test (Table 4.45) show that differences between ME *vs.* MUE are not significant but SE women differ significantly from both ME and MUE women. On *n*-Aggression the single employed group has the lowest score and differs significantly from both the married groups. The married groups are similar to each other.

Table 4.43: Mean and S. D. of *n*-Aggression Scores for Married Employed (ME), Married Unemployed (MUE), and Single Employed (SE) groups

	ME	MUE	SE
Mean	11.56	11.88	10.28
S. D.	3.92	3.199	3.147
N	75	75	75

Table 4.44 : Summary table for one way ANOVA on *n*-Aggression Scores

Source of Variation	Sum of Squares	*df*	Variance	*F*	*p*
Between	118.329	2	59.16444		
Within	2472.59	222	11.13778	5.321	0.01
Total	2590.92	224	11.56659		

Table 4.45 : '*t*'-values indicating intergroup differences on *n*-Aggression Scores

	ME *vs.* MUE	MUE *vs.* SE	ME *vs.* SE
t	0.55	3.09	2.20
p	N.S.	0.01	0.05

The results do not confirm the Hypotheses No. 15 which states that Married Employed and Single Employed are likely to score higher on *n*-Aggression as compared to Married Unemployed women.

n-Aggression refers to characteristics like criticising, making fun or take revenge from, get angry and blame others.

Both the married groups appear to be high on such overt expressions of aggression. Most of the items related to aggression refer to external direction of aggression. The married women usually feel a sense of being accepted within the society as compared to single women. It is possible that the apparent difference between the married and single women may be attributable to the fact that one group has external expression of aggression whereas in the other group it may be directed inwards.

Intergroup Differences on Self-Esteem

Prior to presenting results of self-esteem scores it may be clarified that low scores indicate high self-esteem. The self-esteem scores (Table 4.46) of the comparison groups are 17.80 (ME), 20.70 (MUE), and 18.34 (SE). The value of *F* ratio is 16.965, significant beyond 0.01 level (Table 4.47). A view of Table 4.48 shows that differences between ME *vs.* SE groups are not significant but differences between self-esteem of ME *vs.* MUE and MUE *vs.* SE are significant beyond 0.01 level.

Table 4.46: Mean and S. D. of Self-Esteem Scores (High Scores indicate Low Self-Esteem) for Married Employed (ME), Married Unemployed (MUE), and Single Employed (SE) groups

	ME	MUE	SE
Mean	17.80	20.70	18.34
S. D.	3.33	3.52	3.17
N	75	75	75

Table 4.47 : Summary table for one way ANOVA on Self-Esteem, Scores

Source of Variation	Sum of Squares	*df*	Variance	*F*	*p*
Between	356.720	2	178.36000		
Within	2333.92	222	10.51315	16.965	0.01
Total	2690.64	224	12.01179		

Table 4.48 : '*t*'-values indicating intergroup differences on Self-Esteem Scores

	ME *vs.* MUE	MUE *vs.* SE	ME *vs.* SE
t	5.178	4.31	1.01
p	0.01	0.01	N.S.

On self-esteem the MUE women appear to be having lowest self-esteem and married employed seem to be having the highest self-esteem.

However, the difference between married employed women and single employed women is not significant. Thus it can be said that both the employed groups have a higher self-esteem than unemployed.

The results confirm the Hypothesis No. 16 which states that Married Employed and Single Employed women are likely to have higher self-esteem than Married Unemployed Women.

Self-esteem refers to a positive feeling and a positive attitude toward oneself. Persons high on self-esteem consider themselves competent and view their actions and decisions more positively than persons with low self-esteem. In various studies it has been observed that employed women do have a higher self-esteem as compared to unemployed women. The employed women in fact carries the load of two jobs, one of the households and the other outside the home. Ability to manage on both the fronts naturally enhances a sense that they are capable.

Secondly, the job requires the women to move outside and manage various outside matters also like handling banks, major purchases etc. Thus working women take up many extra responsibilities which are usually handled by men in traditional households.

Furthermore, the extra pay brought home by the working women enhances her economic status. Thereby she may gain greater sense of independence and higher status within the family. This also adds to her self-esteem.

Feld (1963) and Hacker (1971) in their studies have reported that personal self-esteem is found to be higher among employed women. Birnbaum (1971) confirms that working professional women whether married or single hold themselves in higher regard and greater sense of self-worth due to her employed status as compared to equally gifted unemployed women. Mackie (1983) also found self-esteem of working wives significantly higher than that of housewives.

The results of the present study are in consonance with their findings. Table 4.49 shows the number of differences which were found to be significant or not, significant for the each pair compared. It is apparent from this table that the Married Unemployed and Single Employed Women are most different from each others as out of total 16 comparisons 11 were significant.

Table 4.49 : Number of Significant Intergroup Differences

Groups	Significant	Not Significant
MW *vs*. MUE	5	11
MUE *vs*. SE	11	5
ME *vs*. SE	5	11

The Married Employed Women have been found to be similar to both Married Unemployed women and Single Employed women on different aspects. It indicates that married employed who play the dual role of a housewife and a worker also, holds a combination of personality characteristics which reflect aspects of both these roles.

Comparison of High and Low Scorers on n-Achievement within Each Group

The 25 per cent scoring highest on *n*-Achievement (Hn Ach group) and 25 per cent scoring lowest on *n*-Achievement (Ln Ach group) were selected on the basis of overall *n*-Achievement scores. Among the Hn Ach group there were 15 Married Employed, 10 Married Unemployed and 27 Single Employed. Among the Ln Ach group there were 18 Married Employed, 37 Married Unemployed and 5 Single Employed (Table 4.50). The χ^2 computed on this data was equal to 30.48 ($p<0.01$). It indicates that significantly larger number of Single Employed and lower number of Married Unemployed fell into the Hn Ach group. Further, it could be seen that significantly higher number of Married Unemployed and lower number of Single Employed fell into the Ln Ach group. In the Married Employed group the distribution was almost equal to the expectancy value. This further subtantiates the fact that a larger number of Single Employed have high *n*-Achievement and a larger number of Married Unemployed have Ln Ach.

The high and low scorers on *n*-Achievement within each group were compared using '*t*' test (Table 4.53). The Means are given in Tables 4.51 and 4.52 and the '*t*' values are given in Table 4.53. Results indicate that among married employed women Hn Ach and Ln Ach are not very different from each other. Differences in means can be observed only on *n*-Intraception, *n*-Change and *n*-Aggression with Hn Ach group - scoring lower on *n*-Aggression, *n*-Change, and *n*-Intraception. However, differences are significant at 0.05 level only for *n*-Change.

Within the MUE group there appears to be greater variation between Hn Ach and Ln Ach groups. Hn Ach Married Unemployed women have significantly higher mean scores on *n*-Dominance and significantly lower scores on *n*-Order and *n*-Nurturance than Ln Ach Married Employed Women. They also have higher levels of *n*-Deference and lower levels of *n*-Affiliation, *n*-Intraception, *n*-Succourance, *n*-Change, *n*-Eudurance, *n*-Aggression and Self-Esteem as compared to Ln Ach Married Unemployed Women but these differences are significant only at 0.20 level.

Within the Single Employed group also it appears that Hn Ach and Ln Ach differ on various needs. Hn Ach within Single Employed women are significantly higher on *n*-Deference and lower on *n*-Affiliation, *n*-Dominance, and *n*-Nurturance.

Table 4.50: Number and Percentage of High and Low Scores on *n*-Achievement within each Group

	ME	MUE	SE	Total
High *n*-Ach	15 (28.85%)	10 (19.23%)	27 (51.92%)	52
Low *n*-Ach	18 (30%)	37 (61.67%)	5 (8.33%)	60

χ^2 = 30.48 (Calculated on numbers) $p = 0.01$

Table 4.51: Mean and S.D. of Need Scores and Self-Esteem Scores (for Self-Esteem, higher Scores indicates Low Self-Esteem) for High Scorers on *n*-Achievement

(Hn Ach)

Needs & Self-Est	Mean & S.D.	ME (N=15)	MUE (N=10)	SE (N=27)
1	2	3	4	5
Def	M	13.20	14.10	14.33
	S.D.	2.426	2.77	3.93
Ord	M	15.33	12.90	15.07
	S.D.	1.66	4.53	3.09
Exh	M	10.40	13.10	11.59
	S.D.	2.61	3.57	2.51
Aut	M	14.67	13.60	16.07
	S.D.	3.77	2.46	2.70
Aff	M	14.47	13.60	14.67
	S.D.	3.89	1.95	2.40
Int	M	13.33	12.50	13.63
	S.D.	2.79	2.32	2.99
Suc	M	12.60	12.20	13.33
	S.D.	3.16	2.04	3.05
Dom	M	11.66	15.90	13.07
	S.D.	3.45	5.17	3.39
Aba	M	15.13	14.90	14.15
	S.D.	3.05	2.88	3.02
Nur	M	17.73	16.90	16.56
	S.D.	2.52	2.60	2.19
Cha	M	14.27	15.70	13.81
	S.D.	2.52	2.40	3.15

1	2	3	4	5
End	M	17.27	14.40	17.78
	S.D.	4.21	2.67	3.14
Het	M	7.80	8.90	5.74
	S.D.	3.93	1.91	3.18
Agg	M	10.40	10.90	9.15
	S.D.	3.62	2.28	3.17
Self-Est	M	16.80	22.00	17.81
	S.D.	2.68	3.12	2.64

Table 4.52: Mean and S.D. of Need Scores and Self-Esteem Scores (for Self-Esteem, High Scores indicates Low Self-Esteem) for Low Scorers in *n*-Achievement

(Ln Ach)

Needs & Self-Est	Mean & S.D.	ME (N=18)	MUE (N=37)	SE (N=5)
Def	M	13.20	14.10	14.33
Def	M	13.44	12.32	9.40
	S.D.	2.68	2.69	1.10
Ord	M	16.05	16.43	13.20
	S.D.	3.64	3.59	3.27
Exh	M	11.16	12.84	10.20
	S.D.	2.33	2.90	1.92
Aut	M	15.50	14.78	18.00
	S.D.	2.77	3.73	2.12
Aff	M	14.61	14.81	18.80
	S.D.	4.49	2.196	3.49
Int	M	15.22	14.05	12.40
	S.D.	3.89	3.46	2.83
Suc	M	13.11	15.14	13.80
	S.D.	4.83	4.91	3.63
Dom	M	11.66	11.59	16.40
	S.D.	2.72	4.51	2.88
Aba	M	15.94	15.51	15.40
	S.D.	2.44	2.456	2.30
Nur	M	18.33	19.13	20.80
	S.D.	3.56	2.63	3.03
Cha	M	16.22	16.68	14.80
	S.D.	2.86	2.698	4.97
End	M	17.90	16.297	16.80
	S.D.	4.65	4.43	3.11
Het	M	7.78	8.38	6.60
	S.D.	3.82	2.85	2.41
Agg	M	12.56	12.10	12.00
	S.D.	4.245	2.32	2.345
Self-Est	M	16.33	20.95	20.20
	S.D.	3.7	2.95	1.30

Table 4.53 : '*t*' Values indicating differences between High and Low Scorers on *n*-Achievement within each group

Needs & Self-Est	ME (*df*=31)		MUE (*df*=45)		SE (*df*=30)	
	t	*p*	*t*	*p*	*t*	*p*
Def	0.267	N.S.	1.84	0.10	2.75	0.01
Def	0.267	N.S.	1.84	0.10	2.75	0.01
Ord	0.705	N.S.	2.605	0.05	1.238	N.S.
Exh	0.887	N.S.	0.239	N.S.	1.16	N.S.
Aut	0.728	N.S.	0.944	N.S.	1.51	0.20
Aff	0.094	N.S.	1.5796	0.20	3.304	0.01
Int	1.57	0.20	1.336	0.20	0.854	N.S.
Suc	0.351	N.S.	1.84	0.10	0.308	N.S.
Dom	0	N.S.	2.596	0.05	2.06	0.05
Aba	0.848	N.S.	0.67	N.S.	0.874	N.S.
Nur	0.547	N.S.	2.39	0.05	3.75	0.01
Cha	2.06	0.05	1.04	N.S.	0.59	N.S.
End	0.404	N.S.	1.29	N.S.	0.64	N.S.
Het	0.01	N.S.	0.54	N.S.	0.57	N.S.
Agg	1.55	0.20	1.46	0.20	1.905	0.10
Self-Esteem	0.4034	N.S.	0.99	N.S.	1.96	0.10

Differences through only significantly at 0.20 level were found on some of the other aspects also. Hn Ach Single Employed had higher levels on *n*-Order, n-Exhibition and Self-Esteem and lower levels of *n*-Autonomy and *n*-Aggression in comparison to Ln Ach Single Employed Women.

The results related to comparison of high and low scorers on *n*-Achievement presents some interesting findings. Firstly, the Hn Ach and Ln Ach within the married employed group do not appear to the different from each other except on *n*-Change, with Ln Ach having higher scores on *n*-Change.

The high and low scorers on *n*-Achievement appear to be more different within the Married Unemployed and Single Employed groups. Hn Ach among the Married Unemployed have significantly lower on *n*-Order and *n*-Nurturance and they score higher on *n*-Dominance. Even on *n*-Affiliation, *n*-Intraception and *n*-Succourance Hn Ach Married Employed Women have lower scores. Though the '*t*' values are not significant at 0.05 level.

Nurturance, Order, Succourance, Affiliation, Intraception are needs which would be expected to be higher in a homemaker role. The fact that these needs are lower among the Married Unemployed with high need Achievement would indicate that these women would not necessarily be very well adjusted in their present role. They may be happier in a career role. A number of unemployed women did express a desire to take up a profession in the Interview session (Table 4.99).

Within the Single Employed group also the high and low scores on *n*-Achievement appear to be differing on various needs. The Hn Ach Single Women appear to be having higher scores on *n*-Deference, lower scores on *n*-Affiliation, *n*-Dominance, *n*-Nurturance and *n*-Aggression. Here again lower scores on *n*-Affiliation, and *n*-Nurturance among Hn Ach Single Employed Women would indicate that such women would be satisfied within their present role which does not make demands upon them that lower levels of these needs would interfere with their role enactment. The Hn Ach Single Employed Women also appear to be having higher Self-Esteem (lower Self-Esteem score), than the Ln Ach Single Employed who have higher *n*-Nurturance and *n*-Affiliation which cannot be easily satisfied within their present role.

It may be noted that Ln Ach Single Employed have higher score on *n*-Heterosexuality than the Hn Ach Single Employed Women, even though the difference is not significant.

Intergroup Differences within High Scorers and Low Scorers on n-Achievement

Comparisons were made within the high scorers on *n*-Achievement between the various groups (Table 4.54). Among the Hn Ach subjects Married Unemployed Women had higher scores on *n*-Exhibition, *n*-Dominance and they had lower Self-Esteem in comparison to Married Employed Women.

Married Unemployed with high scores on *n*-Achievement had lower scores on *n*-Autonomy and *n*-Endurance and they have lower Self-Esteem as compared to Single Employed Women.

The Hn Ach married employed and single employed did not differ on various needs and Self-Esteem.

The Mean and SDs of Married Employed, Married Unemployed and Single Employed having low scores on *n*-Achievement have been presented in Table 4.52 and '*t*' values indicating differences between various groups have been presented in Table 4.55.

Among Ln Ach subjects the Married Employed appear to be having lower Mean scores on *n*-Exhibition and higher Self-Esteem as compared to Married Unemployed Women.

The Ln Ach Married Unemployed appear to be having significantly lower scores on *n*-Dominance and *n*-Nurturance.

The Ln Ach Married Employed have significantly higher scores on *n*-Deference and lower scores on *n*-Dominance. They also have better Self-Esteem than Single Employed Women scoring lower on *n*-Achievement.

Table 4.54: 't' Values indicating intergroup differences within High Scorers on *n*-Achievement (Hn Ach)

Needs & Self-Est	ME (df = 23)		MUE (df = 35)		SE (df = 40)	
	t	*p*	*t*	*p*	*t*	*p*
Def	0.859	N.S.	0.1613	N.S.	1.008	N.S.
Ord	1.908	0.10.	1.667	0.20	0.3016	N.S.
Exh	2.18	0.05	1.444	0.20	1.4498	0.20
Aut	0.7903	N.S.	2.5258	0.05	1.395	0.20
Aff	0.651	N.S.	1.2593	N.S.	0.2066	N.S.
Int	0.776	N.S.	1.0776	N.S.	0.3188	N.S.
Suc	0.353	N.S.	1.0799	N.S.	0.73	N.S.
Dom	2.46	0.05	1.945	0.10	1.28	N.S.
Aba	0.188	N.S.	0.6782	N.S.	1.003	N.S.
Nur	0.7966	N.S.	0.3988	N.S.	1.57	0.20
Cha	1.413	0.20	1.713	0.10	0.484	N.S.
End	1.90	0.10	3.0146	0.01	0.4455	N.S.
Het	0.82	N.S.	2.95	0.05	1.85	0.10
Agg	0.387	N.S.	1.5928	0.20	1.164	0.20
Self-Esteem	4.4509	0.01	4.0806	0.01	1.183	0.10

Table 4.55 : '*t*' Values indicating intergroup differences within Low Scorers on *n*-Achievement (Ln Ach)

Needs & Self-Est	ME (*df* = 53)		MUE (*df* = 40)		SE (*df* = 21)	
	t	*p*	*t*	*p*	*t*	*p*
Def	1.45	0.20	1.228	N.S.	3.242	0.01
Ord	0.366	N.S.	1.901	0.10	1.579	0.20
Exh	2.14	0.05	1.965	0.10	0.84	N.S.
Aut	0.726	N.S.	1.88	0.10	1.86	0.10
Aff	0.2228	N.S.	3.55	0.01	1.917	0.10
Int	1.129	N.S.	1.016	N.S.	1.502	0.20
Suc	1.45	0.20	0.585	N.S.	0.295	N.S.
Dom	0.0604	N.S.	2.30	0.05	3.41	0.01
Aba	0.6108	N.S.	0.0945	N.S.	0.443	N.S.
Nur	0.9407	N.S.	1.312	0.20	1.408	0.20
Cha	0.5819	N.S.	1.314	0.20	1.15	N.S.
End	1.2407	N.S.	0.244	N.S.	0.495	N.S.
Het	0.65	N.S.	1.31	0.20	0.648	N.S.
Agg	0.5213	N.S.	0.0103	N.S.	0.280	N.S.
Self-Esteem	4.9597	0.01	0.5565	N.S.	2.21	0.05

Among the Hn Ach subjects the Married Employed and Single Employed groups again emerge as having higher Self-Esteem as compared to the Married Unemployed group but not so among subjects scoring low on *n*-Achievement. Here the Married Employed still appear to be having high Self-Esteem but Married Unemployed and Single Employed have low Self-Esteem.

Furthermore, it can also be observed that among the High scores on *n*-Achievement the Married Employed and Single Employed groups are more similar and both these employed groups differ from the unemployed group on various needs.

Married Unemployed women appear to be different from Married Employed women on *n*-Exhibition, *n*-Dominance and Self-Esteem and from Single Employed women on *n*-Autonomy, *n*-Endurance and *n*-Heterosexuality.

Married Unemployed Women having high level of *n*-Achievement also have the highest scores on *n*-Exhibition, *n*-Dominance, *n*-Change and lowest scores on *n*-Order, *n*-Intraception and *n*-Edurance.

A woman in a homemaker role would not find avenues to satisfy a high *n*-Achievement specially in male dominated areas which have been covered in the questionnaire. Furthermore, the opportunity to show off her abilities (*n*-Exhibition) and to make others accept her viewpoint or dominate on others (*n*-Dominance) may also be fewer.

The homemaker role would require them to be more orderly and be able to bear the pressure of routine activities day in and day out. Thus, lower need for order and *n*-Endurance also go against the requirements of a homemaker role.

The homemaker role also does not present a situation where new experiences, new activities may be a part of daily life pattern. All this would lead a woman in a homemaker role with high *n*-Achievement, high *n*-Exhibition, *n*-Dominance and *n*-Change and lower on *n*-Order, *n*-Intraception and *n*-Endurance to remain dissatisfied and hold negative views about herself and her role. This in turn may lead to lower Self-Esteem.

Among the Married Unemployed women with high *n*-Achievement the results do show similar findings.

Among the women with low need for Achievement apart from Self-Esteem the married women appear to be more similar to each other and both married groups differ from the single employed group on various needs. It may be noted that the Single Employed have Self-Esteem scores similar to Married Unemployed women and significantly higher than Married Employed indicating lower Self-Esteem. The Single Employed have a significantly higher *n*-Affiliation and *n*-Dominance.

The scores on *n*-Nurturance are also highest. A Single Employed Women with a low *n*-Achievement and a high *n*-Affiliation is likely to be a misfit within her present role. The role of the working women would provide ample opportunity for Achievement related activities especially in the academic setting it would be possible to write papers, books, works on research projects of high standards but persons lacking *n*-Achievement will not be able to exploit these opportunities. Furthermore, the Affiliative need would have lower chances of satisfaction in this role especially if the women is of a highly dominant temperament.

It would be then expected that these women have few chances of enhancing their Self-Esteem. The results of this study also appear to be in this direction.

The Married Employed women even with low *n*-Achievement may not find it difficult to maintain a high level of Self-Esteem because firstly it is possible that their Achievement goals may be different from those incorporated in the questionnaire. Furthermore, since these women are not very different from the total group on needs like Deference, Affiliation, Succourance and are in fact slightly higher than the average group on needs like Order, Intraception, Nurturance, Endurance and lower on Dominance they may be successful within their homemaker role which may contribute to the maintenance of a higher Self-Esteem which has been found in the results of the present study.

Comparative Study of Subjects with High Self-Esteem (HS EST) and Low Self-Esteem (LS EST)

25 per cent subjects having highest score and 25 per cent subjects having lowest scores on self-esteem were selected from each of the comparison groups on the basis of overall group scores. Number and percentage of subjects falling within each category from each group have been presented in Table 4.56. It is apparent from the table that with $\chi^2 = 29.33$ ($p<0.01$) a significantly higher number of subjects from the married employed and single employed have fallen in the High Self-Esteem Category as compared to Married unemployed group.

The Mean and SDs of need scores of High Self-Esteem subjects have been given in Table 4.57 and for Low Self-Esteem subjects in Table 4.58.

Differences on various needs between High Self-Esteem and Low Self-Esteem subjects within each group were calculated using '*t*' test and results have been presented in Table 4.59. On needs like Achievement, Deference, Exhibition, Autonomy, Affiliation, Succourance, Abasement, Nurturance, Change, Heterosexuality and Aggression differences were not found significant within any of the groups.

Table 4.56 : Number and Percentage of High and Low Self-Esteem Subjects within each group

	ME	MUE	SE	Total
High Self-Esteem Subjects	26 (44.82%)	10 (17.24%)	22 (37.93%)	58
Low Self-Esteem	9 (16.98%)	36 (67.92%)	8 (15.09%)	53

$\chi^2 = 29.33$ (Calculated on numbers) $p < 0.01$

Table 4.57: Mean and S.D. of Need Scorers for High Self-Esteem Subjects (HS Est)

Needs &	Mean & S.D.	ME (N=26)	MUE (N=10)	SE (N=22)
Def	M	13.20	14.10	14.33
Ach	M	15.08	13.00	18.09
	S.D.	3.49	4.47	1.95
Def	M	14.31	12.10	13.45
	S.D.	2.36	2.64	3.51
Ord	M	14.35	12.90	14.64
	S.D.	3.37	4.79	4.80
Exh	M	10.54	13.70	12.05
	S.D.	2.44	2.36	3.11
Aut	M	14.04	14.20	15.82
	S.D.	3.78	2.25	2.95
Aff	M	14.69	15.90	14.36
	S.D.	4.16	2.88	2.34
Int	M	13.31	13.10	12.41
	S.D.	2.82	2.85	2.50
Suc	M	13.46	14.00	12.14
	S.D.	3.43	5.25	4.83
Dom	M	12.96	15.90	14.00
	S.D.	2.12	4.79	3.42
Aba	M	15.58	16.10	13.95
	S.D.	2.90	3.45	2.62
Nur	M	18.19	17.00	17.68
	S.D.	2.86	4.50	2.47
Cha	M	15.38	16.50	15.27
	S.D.	3.84	2.64	3.29
End	M	17.54	14.10	17.45
	S.D.	5.29	4.36	3.45
Het	M	8.12	9.40	7.23
	S.D.	3.76	2.91	3.07
Agg	M	11.12	11.90	10.68
	S.D.	4.10	3.69	3.38

Table 4.58 : Mean aned S.D. of Need Scores for Low Self-Esteem Subjects (LS Est)

Needs &	Mean & S.D.	ME (N=9)	MUE (N=36)	SE (N=8)
Ach	M	15.00	13.50	16.75
	S.D.	2.96	4.06	3.15
Def	M	12.89	12.72	13.25
	S.D.	2.67	2.49	3.95
Ord	M	13.78	15.47	17.13
	S.D.	4.02	2.95	2.90
Exh	M	11.78	12.72	10.25
	S.D.	2.05	2.995	2.37
Aut	M	15.89	14.50	15.25
	S.D.	2.47	3.74	3.88
Aff	M	14.78	14.42	13.88
	S.D.	2.63	3.02	5.34
Int	M	16.00	14.11	14.75
	S.D.	3.46	3.30	2.55
Suc	M	12.22	12.25	14.00
	S.D.	3.27	4.59	1.77
Dom	M	11.89	11.67	15.13
	S.D.	3.59	4.12	3.52
Aba	M	14.22	14.97	13.13
	S.D.	2.11	2.35	2.90
Nur	M	17.67	18.14	17.50
	S.D.	3.16	3.07	1.49
Cha	M	15.33	16.22	11.63
	S.D.	4.44	3.06	2.77
End	M	17.22	16.80	20.25
	S.D.	4.12	3.76	1.39
Het	M	8.44	8.94	5.88
	S.D.	3.09	2.52	2.79
Agg	M	12.22	12.36	10.63
	S.D.	4.02	3.09	2.88

It may be observed that the HS Est subjects within Married Employed group differed significantly from LS Est subjects on *n*-Intraception only. LS Est subjects have significantly higher mean score (M 16.00) than HS Est subjects (M 13.31).

Married Employed LS Est subjects also had lower mean scores on *n*-Deference and higher mean scores on *n*-Exhibition and *n*-Autonomy but the differences were significant only at 0.20 level.

Table 4.59: '*t*' **Values indicating intergroup differences between High and Low Self-Esteem Subjects within each group**

Needs	ME ($df = 33$)		MUE ($df = 44$)		SE ($df = 2$)	
	t	*p*	*t*	*p*	*t*	*p*
Ach	0.06	N.S.	0.34	N.S.	1.41	0.20
Def	1.51	0.20	0.69	N.S.	0.14	N.S.
Ord	0.42	N.S.	2.10	0.05	1.35	0.20
Exh	1.36	0.20	0.95	N.S.	1.49	0.20
Aut	1.37	0.20	0.24	N.S.	0.43	N.S.
Aff	0.06	N.S.	1.75	0.10	0.35	N.S.
Int	2.34	0.05	0.88	N.S.	2.26	0.05
Suc	0.95	N.S.	1.03	N.S.	1.04	N.S.
Dom	0.86	N.S.	2.77	0.01	0.79	N.S.
Aba	1.29	N.S.	1.21	N.S.	0.74	N.S.
Nur	0.46	N.S.	0.93	N.S.	0.09	N.S.
Cha	0.03	N.S.	0.26	N.S.	2.02	0.10
End	0.16	N.S.	1.94	0.10	2.22	0.05
Het	0.23	N.S.	0.94	N.S.	1.09	N.S.
Agg	0.69	N.S.	0.40	N.S.	0.04	N.S.

Within the Married Employed group differences between High Self-Esteem and Low Self-Esteem subjects were significant on *n*-Order and *n*-Dominance. On *n*-Order the LS Est Married Unemployed had significantly higher score (M 15.47) than HS Est subjects (M 12.90). On *n*-Dominance the LS Est married Unemployed subjects have a significantly lower mean score (M 11.67) than HS Est subjects (M 15.90).

Differences between HS Est and LS Est married unemployed have been observed on *n*-Affiliation and *n*-Endurance also but these are only significantly at 0.10 level. LS Est subjects have lower mean score on *n*-Affiliation and higher mean score on *n*-Endurance.

The HS Est and LS Est subjects within single Employed group differed significantly on *n*-Intraception and *n*-Endurance only. The LS Est subjects have scored higher (M 14.75) than HS Est subjects (M 12.41) on *n*-Intraception. On *n*-Endurance also, the LS Est subjects (M 20.25) have a higher mean score than HS Est subjects (M 17.45).

The LS Est Single Employed women also have lower mean

scores on *n*-Achievement, *n*-Exhibition, *n*-Change and higher mean score on *n*-Order but the level of significance is rather low.

It appears from the results that within the two married groups the high and low Self-Esteem subjects were more similar than within the Single Employed group.

The Married Employed with Lower Self-Esteem appear to be more intraceptive, less deferent, more exhibitionistic and desiring greater autonomy. It is possible that these women may be dissatisfied with their housewife role due to their being less deferent and wanting greater autonomy or freedom to act on their own. Many a time women take up jobs since they desire to do so but they may fail to get family support. In these circumstances she is likely to suffer from conflict at home and in her career role also leading to lower levels of Self-Esteem. A number of the Married Employed have expressed dissatisfaction with the amount of help they receive at home from others (Table 4.81), desire to leave the job (Table 4.94), inability to attend the job properly due to home responsibilities (Table 4.86).

The Low Self-Esteem Married Unemployed Women are less dominant, more enduring and more concerned with order. A combination of personality characteristics which would make them very much suitable for the stereotypic role of the housewife. A person who readily takes to the daily drudgery of the household chores, keeps the house in proper order remains submissive. But the low level of need affiliation would result in low interaction with others in the home. A person is happy and satisfied only if he or she feels appreciated by others for whatever he or she is able to accomplish. This low need for affiliation may lead to lowering of this type of feedback from others which is considered to be important for enhancement of Self-Esteem and thus result in low Self-Esteem.

The Single Employed Women with lower Self-Esteem are less achievement oriented, less exhibitionistic, having lower desire for change, more enduring, more intraceptive, and more concerned with order. It is natural that a woman with lower desire for achievement and having characteristics like endurance and intraception will find the role of single career women less satisfying. The most important thing in the life of the single women is the career and a low need for achievement would lead to less interest in activities related with the career role. On the other hand higher level of intraception would mean that such a person would be more interested in knowing and meeting other people. The life of a Single Women in the Indian setting is rather lonely. They may be giving alone at times with few opportunities for socializing. These conditions are likely to lead to a lower level of Self-Esteem.

Intergroup Differences within High Self-Esteem and Low Self-Esteem Subjects

The Mean and S.Ds of High Self-Esteem subjects have been presented in Table 4.57 and '*t*' values indicating differences on various needs among the three comparison groups have been given in Table 4.60. The results presented in the tables suggest that none of the '*t*' values are significant on needs like Order, Autonomy, Affiliation, Intraception, Nurturance, Change, Heterosexuality and Aggression. On *n*-Achievement the differences in MUE *vs*. SE, and ME *vs.* SE are significant. On *n*-Deference difference between MUE and ME are significant. On *n*-Exhibition differences between MUE and ME are significant. On *n*-Succourance significant difference has been found between MUE and SE group only. On *n*-Dominance difference between MUE and ME have been found to be significant. On *n*-Abasement differences between ME and SE are significant.

For subjects lower in Self-Esteem the mean scores on various needs have been given on Table 4.58 and '*t*' value indicating differences on various needs among these groups have been given on Table 4.61. It may be seen that none of the differences are significant on *n*-Deference, *n*-Order, *n*-Autonomy, *n*-Affiliation, *n*-Intraception, *n*-Succourance, *n*-Abasement, *n*-Nurturance and *n*-Aggression. No differences between MUE *vs.* ME are significant. Differences between MUE *vs.* SE groups are significant on *n*-Achievement, *n*-Dominance, *n*-Change and n-Heterosexuality. No significant differences exists between ME and SE groups.

Table 4.60 : '*t*' Values indicating intergroup differences within High Self-Esteem Subjects

Needs	ME *vs.* MUE (*df* = 43)		MUE *vs.* SE (*df* = 30)		ME *vs.* SE (*df* = 46)	
	t	*p*	*t*	*p*	*t*	*p*
Ach	1.50	0.10	4.43	0.01	3.72	0.01
Def	2.46	0.05	1.08	N.S.	1.05	N.S.
Ord	1.03	N.S.	0.95	N.S.	0.24	N.S.
Exh	3.55	0.01	1.46	0.10	1.96	0.10
Aut	0.13	N.S.	1.50	0.10	1.85	0.10
Aff	0.85	N.S.	1.57	0.10	0.34	N.S.
Int	0.20	N.S.	0.68	N.S.	1.20	N.S.
Suc	0.36	N.S.	5.17	0.01	1.04	N.S.
Dom	2.17	0.05	1.25	N.S.	1.14	N.S.
Aba	0.46	N.S.	1.90	0.10	2.09	0.05
Nur	0.95	N.S.	0.54	N.S.	0.68	N.S.
Cha	0.85	N.S.	1.03	N.S.	0.11	N.S.
End	1.84	0.20	2.34	0.05	0.07	N.S.
Het	0.98	N.S.	1.81	0.10	0.89	N.S.
Agg	0.52	N.S.	0.92	N.S.	0.40	N.S.

Table 4.61 : '*t*' Values indicating intergroup differences within Low Self-Esteem Subjects

Needs	ME *vs.* MUE (*df* = 43)		MUE *vs.* SE (*df* = 42)		ME *vs.* SE (*df* = 15)	
	t	*p*	*t*	*p*	*t*	*p*
Ach	1.04	N.S.	2.12	0.05	1.18	N.S.
Def	0.18	N.S.	0.48	N.S.	0.22	N.S.
Ord	1.43	0.20	1.44	0.20	1.94	0.10
Exh	0.89	N.S.	2.18	0.05	1.43	0.20
Aut	1.05	N.S.	0.51	N.S.	0.41	N.S.
Aff	0.33	N.S.	0.39	N.S.	0.45	N.S.
Int	1.52	0.20	0.51	N.S.	0.84	N.S.
Suc	0.02	N.S.	1.05	N.S.	1.37	0.20
Dom	0.15	N.S.	2.19	0.05	1.88	0.10
Aba	0.87	N.S.	1.92	0.10	0.89	N.S.
Nur	0.41	N.S.	0.57	N.S.	0.14	N.S.
Cha	0.71	N.S.	3.92	0.01	2.03	0.10
End	0.29	N.S.	2.54	0.05	1.33	N.S.
Het	0.505	N.S.	3.02	0.01	1.79	0.10
Agg	0.11	N.S.	1.45	0.20	0.93	N.S.

Women having high Self-Esteem do not differ from each other on many needs. However, on *n*-Achievement the single employed group has a very high score and differ significantly from both MUE and ME groups. When the total groups were compared it was found that both the employed groups were similar and the unemployed group had the significantly lower *n*-Achievement score. The picture here seems to be somewhat different with the married groups being similar and the single group being different. It is possible that single women for whom the highest priority is their job and achievement related activities also have a higher Self-Esteem due to consonance with the role expectation.

Single women who have lower *n*-Achievement may not necessarily be comfortable within the role framework of their single status. In fact difference between the *n*-Achievement scores of high self-esteem and low self-esteem subjects confirms the possibility of this conclusion.

The married employed appear to be more deferent, less exhibitionistic, less dominant than married unemployed. Furthermore, they are quite similar to Married Unemployed on needs like Affiliation, Succourance, Abasement, Nurturance and Heterosexuality. It would appear that the HS Est Married Employed women possess characteristics related to housewife role in greater abundance or similar to the housewife themselves. In the Indian setting, the women are only on the verge of emerging from their conventional role setting. Hence while playing the dual role those who are emerging with a personality which may fit with both the roies adequately would feel the greatest sense of success which would reflect in a high level of Self-Esteem.

Among the low Self-Esteem subjects it is interesting to note that Married Employed women appear to be similar to both Married Employed and Single Employed women on most of the need related aspects as the '*t*' values are not significant.

The Married Unemployed appear to be less achievement oriented, more exhibitionistic, less dominant, having greater desire for change, less enduring and higher on Heterosexuality than Single Employed women. Differences between these groups had appeared in the total group scores also and hence the results reflect the fact that low Self-Esteem women are comparatively similar to each other and if differences do occur they reflect the differences in the general population.

Relationship between Need Patterns of the Three Groups

The Mean scores on various needs were ranked for each group and rank order correlation was calculated among the ranks of the needs for the three groups Married Employed, Married Unemployed and Single Employed.

A perusal of the Table 4.62 and the rank order correlations (Table 4.63) present some interesting findings. Similarity among all the three groups is present in rank order for *n*-Nurturance, *n*-Deference, *n*-Exhibition, *n*-Affiliation, *n*-Endurance, *n*-Abasement, *n*-Heterosexuality and *n*-Aggression. Nurturance appears to be the highest ranking need for all the three groups and Heterosexuality appears to be lowest ranking.

Endurance is placed at second (ME and SE) and third (MUE) ranks. Affiliation and Abasement are placed at ranks ranging from 5-7, thus, falling in the middle position of the need patterns. Deference, Exhibition and Aggression stand at the lower end of the need patterns.

On certain needs the ranked position for Married Employed and Single Employed groups are similar. These are Achievement and Succourance, with Achievement being placed at a much higher rank for Married Employed and Single Employed groups (4) than Married Unemployed group (10). On the other hand Succourance has been placed at a much lower rank (11) for both Married Employed and Single Employed group than Married Unemployed (4).

Similarities in the ranked positions of some of the needs like Autonomy, Intraception, Dominance, Change can be observed for the two married groups – Married Employed and Married Unemployed. Autonomy and Dominance have a much higher rank for the Single Employed group (3 and 8 respectively) than for Married Employed and Married Unemployed groups. Conversely *n*-Intraception and *n*-Change have been much lower rank for the

Single Employed group (12 and 9 respectively) than for the two married group.

Rank order correlation between ranks of various needs for the three groups have been found to be 0.776 ($p<0.01$) for ME *vs.* MUE, 0.83 ($p<0.01$) for ME *vs.* SE, and 0.556 ($p<0.05$) for MUE *vs.* SE.

Table 4.62 : Ranking of Mean Scores of Need Variables for ME, MUE and SE groups

Needs	ME		MUE		SE	
	Mean	Rank	Mean	Rank	Mean	Rank
Ach	15.30	4	13.27	10	15.49	4
Def	13.35	10	12.64	11	13.46	10
Ord	14.58	8	15.14	6	15.186	5
Exh	11.06	14	12.58	12	11.60	13
Aut	14.96	6	14.51	8	16.19	3
Aff	14.81	7	14.87	7	15.10	6
Int	14.28	9	13.36	9	13.38	12
Suc	13.23	11	15.38	4	13.44	11
Dom	12.46	12	12.52	13	14.00	8
Aba	15.05	5	15.32	5	14.40	7
Nur	17.86	1	18.13	1	17.80	1
Cha	15.31	3	16.413	2	13.746	9
End	16.83	2	16.04	3	17.346	2
Het	7.44	15	8.746	15	6.346	15
Agg	11.56	13	11.88	14	10.28	14

Table 4.63 : Rank Order Correlations among Mean Need Scores of ME, MUE and SE groups

	ME *vs.* MUE	MUE *vs.* SE	ME *vs.* SE
r	0.8179	0.639	0.8643
p	0.01	0.05	0.01

These ρ values would indicate greater similarities between ME and SE on one hand and ME and MUE on the other hand. But a comparatively lower level of similarity exists between MUE and SE group. This corroborates with the results of analysis of variance ant '*t*' test in which it had been found that Married Employed are similar to Married Unemployed in certain aspects and similar to Single Employed on certain other aspects.

Analysis of Social Background

Parental Influences

(i) *Educational and Professional Status of Father :* Informations regarding the educational status of fathers of the subjects has been presented in Table 4.64. It can be observed that significantly ($\chi^2 = 39.55, p < 0.01$) larger number of Married Unemployed has fathers educated below graduation (33.33%) as compared to both the employed groups. Only 10.67 per cent of Married Employed and 9.33 per cent of Single Employed had fathers educated below graduation level. Furthermore, very few of the fathers of Married Unemployed (9.33%) had education above graduation in comparison to Married Employed (26.67%) and Single Employed (46.67%). It can, hence, be concluded that fathers of the employed women had higher level of education as compared to fathers of unemployed women.

With regard to the professional status of fathers data has been presented in Table 4.65. Hence, differences are not so marked but a point worth noting is that a larger number of fathers of Married Employed (14.71%) and Single Employed (24.66%) were in teaching profession as compared to Married Unemployed (7.25%). The employed women in the sample consisted of university teachers only, hence, the possibility that their fathers may have played a role in motivating them to go for the teaching profession cannot be denied. In fact 61.33 per cent of Married Employed and 90.67 per cent of Single Employed have reported that they were motivated by their fathers to take the job (Table 4.67).

(ii) *Educational Status of Mother :* Data related to educational status of mothers has been presented in Table 4.66. It may be seen that more of the mothers of Married Employed (8% + 4%) and Single Employed women (20% + 4%) had education above graduation as compared to Married Unemployed women (2.67% + 1.33%). Furthermore it may be seen that mothers of 12 per cent of Married Unemployed women were illiterate whereas only 8 per cent of mothers of Married Employed and 2.67 per cent of mothers of Single Employed were illiterate. Most of the mothers were not in job but it seems possible that these educated mothers may have influenced their daughters in such a way that they may have planned for careers in their adult life.

Table 4.64 : Educational Status of Father

Groups	Below Graduation	Graduation	Above Graduation	Professional	Total	χ^2	p
ME	8 (10.67%)	28 (37.33%)	20 (26.67%)	19 (25.33%)	75		
MUE	25 (33.33%)	26 (34.67%)	7 (9.33%)	17 (22.67%)	75	39.55	0.01
SE	7 (9.33%)	14 (18.67%)	35 (46.67%)	19 (25.33%)	75		

Table 4.65 : Professional Status of Father

Group	Agriculture	Teacher	Professional	Nonprofessional	Totals	χ^2	p
ME	0 0%	10 14.71%	2 2.94%	56 82.35%	68		
MUE	3 4.35%	5 7.25%	9 13.04%	52 75.36%	69	15.58	0.02
SE	2 2.74%	18 24.66%	6 8.22%	47 64.38%	73		

Table 66 : Educational Status of Mother

Group	Illiterate	Literate	Below Graduate	Graduate	Post-Graduate or above	Totals	χ^2	p
ME	6 (8%)	4 (5.33%)	56 (74.67%)	6 (8%)	3 (4%)	75		
MUE	9 (12%)	7 (9.33%)	56 (74.67%)	2 (2.67%)	1 (1.33%)	75	19.09	0.05
SE	2 (2.67%)	3 (4%)	52 (69.33%)	15 (20%)	3 (4%)	75		

(iii) *Father as Motivating Person* : The educational and professional status of the father's of the SS who had listed their fathers as the motivating person has been analyzed. 61.33 per cent of Married Employed women, 90.67 per cent of Single Employed women and 25.58 per cent of Married Unemployed women out of those who had reported that they are motivated by someone had reported being motivated by the fathers. From the data it appears that most of the fathers who motivated their daughters had higher levels of education (Table 4.67) even though they may not have been at a high professional status (Table 4.68). Single Employed appear to be mostly motivated by the fathers.

Table 4.67 : Educational Status of Father's Motivating Subjects to take job

Groups	Below Gradu-ation	Graduation	Above Gradua-tion	Professionals	Totals
ME	6	17	14	9	46 61.33%
MUE	2	3	1	5	11 25.58%
SE	3	16	41	8	68 9067%

Table 4.68 : Professional Status of Father's Motivating Subjects to take job

Groups	Agricul-ture	Teacher	Professional	Non-profe-ssionals	Total
ME	0	8	2	36	46 61.33%
MUE	1	0	5	5	11 25.58%
SE	2	18	5	43	68 90.67%

(iv) *Mother as Motivating Person* : Within the subjects who had listed their mothers as motivating person the Single Employed had the highest frequency (90.67%) followed by Married Employed and Married Unemployed. Many of the mothers of working women were highly educated but a large number had education below graduation. The significant fact was that even though the number of mothers having education below graduation was approximately equal for each of the group. Very few (25.58%) mothers of this or higher educational level had motivated the SS of Married Unemployed group (Table 4.69). Thus it can be said that role of both father and mother may be important as a motivating person for eventual striving for employment.

(v) *Opportunity for Independent Thinking and Movement* : The subjects were asked to report the perceived opportunity for independent thinking and movement given by the parents. They were to pick up from four alternative responses always, very often, often and rarely. The response frequencies are given in Table 4.70. The χ^2 value 18.17 ($p < 0.01$).

Table 4.69 : Educational Status of Mother's Motivating Subjects to take job

Group	Illiterate	Literate	Below Graduate	Graduate	Post-Graduate	Total
ME	5 (10.87%)	0 (0%)	38 (82.61%)	2 (4.35%)	1 (2.17%)	46
MUE	1 (9.09%)	0 (0%)	10 (90.91%)	0 (0%)	0 (0%)	11
SE	0 (0%)	3 (4.41%)	48 (70.59%)	15 (22.06%)	2 (2.94%)	68

Table 4.70 : Opportunity given for Independent thinking and movement

Groups	Always	Very often	Often	Rarely	Total	χ^2	p
ME	48 (64%)	18 (24%)	4 (5.33%)	5 (6.67%)	75		
MUE	65 (86.67%)	6 (8%)	1 (1.33%)	3 (4%)	75	18.17	0.01
SE	65 (86.67%)	9 (12%)	0 (0%)	1 (1.33%)	75		

Interestingly enough fewer of the Married Employed women (64%) have chosen the always category of response as compared to Married Unemployed women (86.67%) and Single Employed Women (86.67%). It would have been expected that the working women would have received more opportunities for independent action but the results are opposite to this assumption. However, a possibility exists that the employed women now required to move out and act independently perceived the opportunities given as being lesser that what would be required to train them for their present life style. Whereas unemployed women who are less exposed to situations demanding independent action may perceive the same opportunities as being more than sufficient.

(vi) *Parents' Attitude about Working Women* : The subjects were asked to report their perception of the attitude of their parents towards working women. The response categories were positive, negative and neutral. Response frequencies and percentages are given in Table 4.71. The Chi square (χ^2) value was found to be 28.23 ($p < 0.01$). It can be seen from the table that most of the Married Employed (69.33%) perceived their parents to be holding positive, 26.67 per cent neutral and only 4 per cent negative attitudes. Among the Single Employed women 40 per cent perceived their parents as holding positive, 60 per cent neutral attitude and none reported a negative attitude. Among the Married Unemployed parents of 44 per cent were perceived to be having positive, 44 per cent neutral and 12 per cent having negative attitude. It is apparent that most of the working women especially the married ones felt that their parents had a positive attitude towards working women. Only a nominal number reported negative attitudes but within the Married Unemployed group fewer reported positive attitudes and some in fact reported negative attitude. It is quite probable that these attitudes of the parents would eventually effect the decisions regarding preparation for a profession and later decision regarding profession.

Table 4.71 : Parents Attitude towards Working Women

Groups	Positive	Negative	Neutral	Total	χ^2	p
ME	52	3	20	75		
	(69.33%)	(4%)	(26.67%)			
MUE	33	9	33			
	(44%)	(12%)	(44%)	75	28.23	0.01
SE	30	0	45			
	(40%)	(0%)	(60%)	75		

(vii) *Important Plans for Future* : The subjects were asked to indicate what their parents held as most important for their future plans. They were given the alternative career, marriage, both equally or any other to choose from. The results have been presented in Table 4.72 for all the three groups.

It is apparent from the table that for a maximum number of Married Employed women, both marriage and career were held equally important by their parents. The Chi square (χ^2) value is 68.59, significant beyond 0.01 level. Most of the parents of both the working groups appear to have held both career and marriage equally important as 74.67 per cent of Married Employed women and 82.67 per cent of SE have chosen the "both equally important" category, in contrast to MUE group where only 41.33 per cent have responded on this category. Further, MUE group has responded to the category 'marriage', maximally (56%), only 1.33 per cent of SE group have chosen this category and 14.67 per cent of ME group have responded on this category. It appears that only 2.67 per cent MUE perceive their parents as considering career important for their future in contrast to 60 per cent from the SE group and 10.67 per cent from ME group. If career and both equally categories are considered together it is apparent that parents of about 75 per cent of ME, 98 per cent of SE and only 44 per cent of MUE had thought of a/career for their daughters.

Table 4.72 : Parental plans for Subject's future

Group	Career	Marriage	Both Equally	Total	χ^2	*p*
ME	8 (10.67%)	11 (14.67%)	56 (74.67%)	75		
MUE	2 (2.67%)	42 (56%)	31 (41.33%)	75	68.59	0.01
SE	12 (16%)	1 (1.33%)	62 (82.67%)	75		

Thus, it is indicated that parents did differ in their future plans for their daughters. It is apparent that most of the parents of working women had in fact shown the idea of a career in the minds of the employed women. Whereas more than 50 per cent of parents of MUE had planned only a marriage for them.

Role of Present Family

(i) *Other Family Members as Motivating Persons* : The employed subjects were asked to report as to who motivated them to take a job and the Married Unemployed who reported planning to take a job were asked to report as to who is motivating them. As discussed earlier, for employed women, parents mostly appear to be the motivating person (Table 4.73). Apart from parents among the married women 52 per cent of ME women and 40 per cent of MUE women have listed their husbands as motivating person. In fact, among the Married Employed women quite a number of subjects had reported both parents and husbands as motivating person but there was no such overlapping among Married Unemployed women.

Table 4.73 : Persons motivating to seek employment

Groups	No one or Myself*	Parents	Husbands	In-laws	Others	Total
ME	16 (21.33%)	46 (61.33%)	39 (52%)	1 (1.33%)	6 (8%)	108
MUE	8 (10.67%)	9 (12%)	30 (40%)	2 (2.67%)	7 (9.33%)	56
SE	7 (9.33%)	68 (90.67%)	0 (0%)	0 (0%)	7 (9.33%)	82

* One subject gave names of more than one person

It is interesting to note that many Married Employed woman (21.33%), Single Employed women (9.33%), and Married Unemployed women (10.67%) have taken the decision to go for a job by themselves indicating a sense of confidence and need for striving for success without any external pressure within women. Furthermore, In-laws have been listed as motivating persons only by 1.33 per cent of ME women and 2.67 per cent of MUE women. It would appear that at least the In-laws do not play a positive role in context to motivating the married women to take a job.

(ii) *Satisfaction of Family Members regarding Present **Employment** Status* : The subjects had to respond to the question "**What** do your family members feel about your present employment status?" The responses were to be given in three categories satisfied, neutral and dissatisfied. The family members listed were husband, children, In-laws and other relatives. The responses of the subject have been presented in Tables 4.74, 4.75, 4.76, 4.77. All Chi square values were significant at 0.01 level.

It can be seen from Table 4.74 that most of the Married Employed (93.33%) reported that their husbands felt satisfied about their present employed status. Whereas only (52%) of MUE felt that their husbands were satisfied with their present housewife status. 46.67 per cent of MUE perceived their husband's attitude as neutral. Thus, it can be said that most of the married employed perceived their husband to be having a positive attitude towards their employed status.

Perceived feeling of the children have been reported in Table 4.75. Here again, it can be seen that 75.81 per cent of Married Employed as against 28.17 per cent of Married Unemployed per-ceived their children to be satisfied with their employment status. It again reflects the fact that children of married employed are more positively disposed towards their mother's employment status.

The perception of satisfaction of in-laws has been reported in Table 4.76. Here again we find that 63.77 per cent of married employed as against 26.39 per cent of Married Unemployed women have reported that their in-laws feel satisfied about their employment status.

Here the neutral response has been reported in 72.22 per cent cases for MUE and 33.33 per cent of ME. Thus it would appear that more of the in-laws are neutral but here again the Married Employed women have an advantage over Married Unemployed women as more of their in-laws appear to be positively satisfied.

Table 4.74 : Husband's Satisfaction with Subjects present Employment Status

Groups	Satisfied	Neutral	Dissatis-fied	Total	χ^2	*p*
ME	70 (93.33%)	3 (4%)	2 (2.67%)	75		
MUE	39 (52%)	35 (46.67%)	1 (1.33%)	75	19.50	0.01

Table 4.75 : Children's Satisfaction with Subjects Present Employment Status

Groups	Satisfied	Neutral	Dissatisfied	Total	χ^2	*p*
ME	47 (75.81%)	13 (20.97%)	2 (3.23%)	62	30.69	0.01
MUE	20 (28.17%)	48 (67.61%)	3 (4.23%)	71		

Table 4.76 : In-laws Satisfaction with Subjects Present Employment Status

Groups	Satisfied	Neutral	Dissatis-fied	Total	χ^2	*p*
ME	44 (63.77%)	23 (38.33%)	2 (2.90%)	69	21.41	0.01
MUE	19 (26.39%)	52 (72.22%)	1 (1.39%)	72		

Table 4.77 : Other Relatives Satisfaction with Subjects Present Employment Status

Groups	Satisfied	Neutral	Dissatis-fied	Total	χ^2	*p*
ME	18 (26.47%)	26 (38.24%)	24 (35.29%)	68		
MUE	19 (25.68%)	52 (70.27%)	3 (4.05%)	74	49.93	0.01
SE	22 (29.73%)	52 (70.27%)	0 (0%)	74		

The responses of the subjects on the question of perceived satisfaction of other relatives regarding the subjects employment status has been given in Table 4.77. A perusal of the table shows that in this case approximately equal number of subjects from each group, MUE (25.68%), ME (26.47%), SE (29.73%), have responded to the category satisfied. Among both married unemployed and single employed women 70.27 per cent have responded to the neutral category whereas only 38.24 per cent of Married Employed women have responded to this category. In fact a large number of ME women 35.29 per cent have responded to the dissatisfied category.

It would, thus, appear that quite a few number of Married Employed women have to face a negative attitude from other relatives, even though, they receive positive support from their immediate relatives like husband, children and in-laws.

Mostly the near relatives of Married Unemployed women are neutral to their employment status *i.e.* being housewife.

(iii) *Help and Support received from Family Members* : The subjects were asked two questions in context to the help and support they receive (Tables 4.78, 4.79, 4.80) and their satisfaction with the amount of help and support (Table 4.81).

If we look at the tables regarding help and support received in household work (Table 4.78) it appears that while 10.67 per cent of married employed women and 70.67 per cent of single employed women report being helped by the parents, none of the Married Unemployed women do so. Approximately equal number of Married Employed women (21.33%) and Married Unemployed women (22.67%) have reported being helped by in-laws, 69.33 per cent of Married Employed women and 79.59 per cent of Married Unemployed women report being helped by their husbands, 48 per cent of Married Employed women and 66.67 per cent of Married Unemployed women report being helped by children. It would appear that with respect to household work Married Unemployed women get more support than Married Employed women or Single Employed women.

In case of children (Table 4.79) 16 per cent of Married Employed women and 1.33 per cent of Married Unemployed women report getting help from parents, equal number of 21.33 per cent of Married Unemployed women and Married Employed women report getting help from in-laws, 65.33 per cent of Married Employed women and 88 per cent of MUE women report getting help from husbands, 4 per cent of ME women and 13.33 per cent of MUE women report getting help from children, 17.33 per cent of ME women and 2.67 per cent MUE women report getting help from others.

Here again it appears that Married Unemployed women get more help and support from their husbands and children whereas Married Employed women get some extra support from parents and others.

Table 4.78 : Help and Support in Household Work from Family Members

Groups	Parents	In-laws	Husband	Children	Others	Total
ME	8 (10.67%)	16 (21.33%)	52 (69.33%)	36 (48%)	53 (70.67%)	75
MUE	0 (0%)	17 (22.67%)	59 (79.59%)	50 (66.67%)	60 (80%)	75
SE	53 (70.67%)	0 (0%)	0 (0%)	0 (0%)	69 (92%)	75

Table 4.79 : Help and Support in Children's Care from Family Members

Groups	Parents	In-laws	Husband	Children	Others	Total
ME	12 (16%)	16 (21.33%)	49 (65.33%)	3 (4%)	13 (17.33%)	75
MUE	1 (1.33%)	16 (21.33%)	66 (88%)	10 (13.33%)	2 (2.67%)	75
SE	—	—	—	—	—	—

Table 4.80 : Help and Support in Outside Rsponsibilities from Family Members

Groups	Parents	In-laws	Husband	Children	Others	Total
ME	5 (6.67%)	7 (9.33%)	62 (82.67%)	6 (8%)	9 (12%)	75
MUE	3 (4%)	15 (20%)	62 (82.67%)	1 (1.33%)	0 (0%)	75
SE	46 (61.33%)	0 (0%)	0 (0%)	0 (0%)	43 (57.33%)	75

Table 4.81 : Satisfaction with the Amount of Help and Support Received

Groups	Yes	No	Total	χ^2	*p*
ME	69 (92%)	6 (8%)	75		
MUE	75 (100%)	0 (0%)	75	6.26	0.05
SE	72 (96%)	3 (4%)	75		

In context to outside responsibilities (Table 4.80) 6.67 per cent of Married Employed women, 61.33 per cent of Single Employed women and 4 per cent of Married Unemployed women receive support from parents. 9.33 per cent of ME women and 20 per cent of MUE women get help from in-laws. 82.67 per cent of both ME women and MUE women report getting help from their husbands, 8 per cent of ME women, 1.33 per cent of MUE women report getting help from children, 12 per cent of ME women, 57.33 per cent of SE women and none of MUE women report getting help from others. The SE women mostly get support from parents or others. More of MUE women appear to be getting help from their in-laws, whereas maximum help is received from husbands which is equal for both ME and MUE women.

On the whole it would appear that Married Employed women and Married Unemployed women get almost equal or at times Married Unemployed women get more support and help from different quarters than ME. Considering the fact that ME women have greater responsibility and probably lesser support than the MUE women who have slightly lesser responsibility are likely to feel less satisfied with the amount of help and support received from various quarters.

With respect to the second question Chi square was found to be 6.26 ($p < 0.05$). The responses of the single employed do not differ from the independence value, hence it is only the variation in the responses of ME and MUE groups which contribute to the Chi square. It appears that all the Married Unemployed women are satisfied with the help and support but 8 per cent of Married Employed are not satisfied with the help and support.

Attitude towards Career Women

(i) *More Respect for Career Women than Housewife* : The subjects were asked whether career women are more respected than housewives. The results are presented in Table 4.82. The Chi square (χ^2) value is 5.07 significant only at 0.10 level. Thus, it is apparent that the three groups have responded in a similar fashion. It can be seen that 96 per cent of ME women, 97.33 per cent of SE women and 89.33 per cent of MUE women have endorsed the statement. A greater number of MUE women (10.67%) have shown disagreement with the statement as compared to ME women (4%) and SE women (2.67%) but the number is not so high that it may be concluded that more housewives disagree with the fact that career women are more respected than housewives.

A large number of them 82.67 per cent (Table 4.99) have actually expressed the desire to take up a job. For various reasons (Tables 4.100 and 4.101) like self-fulfilment, use of high qualification 13.33 per cent, independence 16 per cent, relief from boredom 26.67 per cent, to pass time 13.33 per cent, and money 13.33 per cent.

17.33 per cent did not wish to take a job but one-third of these did not give any reason, one-third had small children, only one-third of these MUE group did not want to take a job because they did not want to do any extra work. The results thus break the myth that women enjoy sitting at home being housewives and do not wish to take outside responsibilities and that they do not have desire for achievement. Most of the educated women do wish to take up employment.

Table 4.82 : Career Women Respected more than Housewives

Groups	Yes	No	Total	χ^2	p
ME	72 (96%)	3 (4%)	75		
MUE	67 (89.33%)	8 (10.67%)	75	5.07	0.10
SE	73 (97.33%)	2 (2.67%)	75		

The housewives, thus, are in a dissonant situation where they have to face the fact that they are housewives but they are less respected than career women and they wish to reduce it by joining a job. This dissonance is possibly reflected in their low self-esteem (Tables 4.46 and 4.48).

(ii) *Career Women is Less Satisfied and Less Happier than the Housewives* : The subjects were asked to agree or disagree with the statement that career women is less satisfied and less happier than the housewives. Results are given in Table 4.83. The calculated Chi square is 6.86 ($p < 0.05$). It can be seen that most of the single employed women have disagreed with the statement. A few (4%) of the ME group have endorsed the statement but most (96%) of them have disagreed. Of the MUE group 10.67 per cent have agreed with the statement. This indicates that more of married women specially the unemployed feel that career women are less satisfied and less happier but the more significant fact is that 89 per cent of MUE group do not feel that the career women is less satisfied or less happier. The findings are in consonance with the above discussion.

Table 4.83 : Career Women Less Satisfied and Less Happier

Groups	Yes	No	Total	χ^2	p
ME	3 (4%)	72 (96%)	75		
MUE	8 (10.67%)	67 (89.33%)	75	6.86	0.05
SE	1 (1.33%)	74 (98.67%)	75		

Table 4.84 : Women should concentrate more on Home than Career

Groups	Yes	No	Both Equally	Total	χ^2	p
ME	11 (14.67%)	33 (44%)	31 (41.33%)	75		
MUE	15 (20%)	23 (30.67%)	37 (49.33%)	75	7.50	0.20
SE	7 (9.33%)	38 (50.67%)	30 (40%)	75		

Home *vs.* Job Conflict

(i) *Women should Concentrate More on Home than Career* : The subjects were asked to express their views in context to the statement that women should concentrate more on home than career. The responses have been presented in Table 4.84. The χ^2 value was not found significant. However, it can be seen from the table that more of married women endorsed the views (ME

14.67%, MUE 20%) as compared to single employed women (9.33%). In contrast, more of single employed women (50.67%) disagreed with the statement as compared to ME women (44%) and MUE women (30.67%). Thus, the single employed women appear to consider career more or equally important to home than the married women.

(ii) *Unable to attend Job due to Home and vice-versa* : The subjects were asked two questions related to inability to attend home responsibilities due to job and job responsibilities due to home. The responses have been given in Tables 4.85 and 4.86 respectively. Chi square χ^2 for both are significant beyond 0.01 level. It can be seen that more of married employed suffer from the conflict between home and job responsibilities. Almost none of the single employed suffer from such a problem.

Table 4.85 : Unable to attend Home properly because of Job

Groups	Often	Rarely	Total	χ^2	*p*
ME	12 (16%)	63 (84%)	75	13.04	0.01
SE	0 (0%)	75 (100%)	75		

Table 4.86 : Unable to attend Job properly because of Home Responsibilities

Groups	Often	Rarely	Total	χ^2	*p*
ME	13 (17.33%)	62 (82.67%)	75	11.34	0.01
SE	1 (1.33%)	74 (98.67%)	75		

Views regarding Job Related Aspects

(i) *Highest Professional Ambition* : The working women were asked to report their highest professional ambition. The alternatives given were professional excellence, academic excellence and any other. 84 per cent of the Married Employed women and 65.3 per cent of the Single Employed responded. Results have been presented in Table 4.87, 42.67 per cent of ME women and 40 per cent of SE women consider professional excellence as their goal.

33.33 per cent of ME women and 25.33 per cent by SE women are directed towards academic excellence.

It is interesting to note that 8 per cent of ME women have given the response nothing. A look into the reasons for taking the job for these women showed that two subjects were working for financial supplementation. One to pass time, one due to chance, one had not given any reason, only one had listed self-fulfilment as a reason. Thus it seems that persons who are working either under external pressures or due to non-significant reasons are likely to be less ambitious.

(ii) *Important Aspects in Job* : The working women were asked to report as to which aspects they thought to be most important in their jobs. They had to choose from three alternatives academic, administrative, and both equally. The results have been presented in Table 4.88. The Chi square is 11.66 ($p < 0.01$). It is apparent that administrative aspect has not been considered so important or to have priority over academic. Subjects have either chosen academic or both equally category. Responses of ME women differs significantly from Single Employed women. A greater number of (49.33%) ME women have given priority to academic aspects as against 22.67 per cent of Single Employed women.

Table 4.87 : Highest Professional Ambition

Groups	Professional Excellence	Academic Excellence	Nothing	Total	χ^2	*p*
ME	32	25	6	63		
	(42.67%)	(33.33%)	(8%)		5.21	0.10
SE	30	19	0	49		
	(40%)	(25.33%)	(0%)			

Note—All percentage out of 75

Table 4.88 : Aspects considered Important in Job

Groups	Academic	Administrative	Both Equally	Total	χ^2	*p*
ME	37	1	37	75		
	(49.33%)	(1.33%)	(49.33%)		11.66	0.01
SE	17	1	57	75		
	(22.67%)	(1.33%)	(76%)			

More of SE subjects (76%) have held both the aspects as being equally important. Single Employed Women have been found to be higher on *n*-Achievement (Tables 4.1 and 4.3) and *n*-Dominance (Tables 4.25 and 4.27), hence the results are in consonance. The reason for Married Employed Women giving less importance to the administrative aspects may be attributable to constraints on time and energy resulting from fulfilling diverse demands for the two roles.

(iii) *Strive for In Job* : The subjects were asked to report what they strived for in their job. The responses to be chosen from were academic success and administrative success. The responses are presented in Table 4.89. The χ^2 is 21.13 ($p < 0.01$). It can be seen that maximum number of Single Employed women (92.42%) strive for administrative success. Whereas only 58.33 per cent of ME Women try to achieve administrative success. A large number of Married Employed (41.67%) work for academic success. In this context it may be remembered that the ME and SE groups do not differ on *n*-Achievement but it is possible that the direction of the need may be different. The ME women who have to balance their time and energy between home and job, more often choose to work for a academic success as it involves, more autonomy in terms of time distribution between the two responsibilities.

Table 4.89 : Strive for in Job

Groups	Academic Success	Administrative Success	Total	χ^2	*p*
ME	30 (41.67%)	42 (58.33%)	72		
				21.13	0.01
SE	5 (8.46%)	61 (92.42%)	66		

(iv) *Regard and Respect from Colleagues* : The SS were asked whether they felt that they received respect and regard from their male and female colleagues. The responses of the subjects have been presented in Tables 4.90 and 4.91. The Chi square (χ^2) are 9.77 for perceived responses of male colleagues ($p < 0.01$) and 4.1 for perceived responses of female colleagues ($p < 0.05$). It can be observed from the tables that significantly more of single employed feel that they are getting regard and respect from both male and female colleagues whereas 28 per cent of Married Employed felt that they were not getting respect and regard from their male colleagues and 5.33 per cent felt the same with respect to female colleagues. A number of Married Employed women are under tension with regard to home and job responsibilities. It is possible that as a result their performance may suffer and this may lead to lesser respect from male colleagues who usually neither have to face such a problem nor can they appreciate the depth of this problem. The single women who have reported not having any problem with respect to handling home and job responsibilities would be able to give more attention to job related activities and hence, earn more respect.

Table 4.90 : Regard and Respect received from Male Colleagues

Groups	Yes	No	Total	χ^2	p
ME	54 (72%)	21 (28%)	75	9.77	0.01
SE	42 (95.45%)	2 (4.55%)	44		

Table 4.91 : Regard and Respect received from Female Colleagues

Groups	Yes	No	Total	χ^2	p
ME	71 (94.67%)	4 (5.33%)	75	4.1	0.05
SE	75 (100%)	0 (0%)	75		

(v) *Satisfaction with the Job* : The employed women were asked to report if they felt satisfied with their jobs. The responses are presented in Table 4.93. Most of the SE women 98.67 per cent responded in affirmative whereas 12 per cent of ME women responded in negative. It appears that even though most of the married women are satisfied with their jobs a few are not, possibly due to home related conflicts (Tables 4.85 and 4.86).

(vi) *Desire to Leave the Job* : The employed subjects were

asked whether they would like to their job if conditions permit. The responses of the subjects have been given in Table 4.94. The Chi square (χ^2) is 17.26 ($p < 0.05$). It is interesting to note that a significantly large number of ME women (26.67%) would like to do so. When the employed subjects were asked to report if they were satisfied with their job 12 per cent of the ME women had responded in negative whereas almost all of the SE women (98.67%) had responded in affirmative (Table 4.93). When the working women were asked to report their reasons for working (Table 4.92) 12 per cent of ME had reported financial reasons and 12 per cent had reported reasons like avoiding boredom, passing time, and 10.67 per cent had reported coming into job by chance. In fact most of the women expressing desire to leave the job were the ones who were working either primarily due to financial pressure or had come into career just by chance or due to boredom or to pass time.

Table 4.92 : Reasons for taking the Job

S. No.	Reasons	Number	
		ME	SE
1.	To be a good researcher & Artist	3 (4%)	4 (5.33%)
2.	Financial help in family	9 (12%)	1 (1.33%)
3.	Independence and Independent Identity	16 (21.33%)	19 (25.33%)
4.	By Chance	8 (10.67%)	5 (6.67%)
5.	Desire and Self-fulfilment	8 (10.67%)	0 (0%)
6.	Interest in teaching	20 (26.67%)	25 (33.33%)
7.	Utilize education and knowledge	2 (2.67%)	2 (2.67%)
8.	Others (No specific reasons, avoid boaringness, to pass time)	9 (12%)	19 (25.33%)
	Total	75	75

Subjects who had taken the job for reasons like being good researchers, independence, self-fulfilment, interest in teaching or reaching a level of excellence in their field preferred to retain their jobs under every condition.

Table 4.93 : Satisfaction with the Job

Groups	Yes	No	Total	χ^2	p
ME	66 (88%)	9 (12%)	75	6.86	0.01
SE	74 (98.67%)	1 (1.33%)	75		

Table 4.94 : Desire to leave the Job

Groups	Yes	No	Total	χ^2	p
ME	20 (26.67%)	55 (73.33%)	75	17.26	0.01
SE	2 (2.67%)	73 (97.33%)	75		

(vii) *Advantages and Disadvantages of being a Working Person*: The working women were asked to report as to what were the advantages and disadvantages of being a working person. The results have been presented in Tables 4.95 and 4.96.

Most of the disadvantages fell into three categories negligence of home and children, extra load due to dual responsibility, lack of time. Only about 34 per cent single employed women reported disadvantages in contrast to about 72 per cent of ME women. Almost all of SE women reporting disadvantages and 34.67 per cent of ME felt that extra load due to dual responsibility was the

Table 4.95 : Disadvantages of being in Employment

Groups	Negligence of Home & Children	Extra load due to dual responsibility	Lack of time	No Disadvantages
ME	24 (32%)	26 (34.67%)	4 (5.33%)	2 (2.67%)
SE	0 (0%)	23 (30.67%)	3 (4%)	0 (0%)

Note—All percentage is out of 75.

greatest problem. However, among the ME women 32 per cent found negligence of home and children as the greatest disadvantage. 5.33 per cent of ME women reported lack of time as the greatest problem and only 2.67 per cent remarked there were no disadvantages. It appears that working women continually suffer from the tension of dual responsibility but the married working women due to responsibility of children suffer most.

With respect to reporting of advantages (Table 4.96) the responses fell into four categories satisfaction due to independence, security (financial), self-development, prestige, 45 per cent of ME women and 50.69 per cent of SE women considered financial security as the greatest advantages. 20 per cent from both the groups considered the satisfaction due to being independent as being most important and 13.33 per cent of ME women and none of SE considered self-development as the greatest advantage of working. Prestige was considered important by 8 per cent of SE women but by none of the ME women. Thus it appears that financial security is considered to be the greatest advantage of taking a job.

Table 4.96 : Advantages of being in Employment

Groups	Satisfaction due to indep-endent	Security (Financial)	Self-Deve-lopment	Prestige
ME	15 (20%)	34 (45.33%)	10 (13.33%)	0 (0%)
SE	15 (20%)	38 (50.67%)	0 (0%)	6 (8%)

(ix) *Financial Security* : The subjects were asked whether they felt financially secure or not. The results have been given in Table 4.97. The Chi square χ^2 is 10.89 ($p < 0.01$). They were also asked if they felt that their and their family's needs were being satisfied within the total family income. The responses are given in Table 4.98 and the Chi square χ^2 value is 19.55 ($p < 0.01$). It can be seen from the tables that all of the SE subjects reported feeling financially secure and satisfied with the total income. Most of the ME group (97.33%) felt financially secure and most (98.67%) thought the family income to be sufficient. However within the

MUE group a significantly greater number (10.66%) reported not feeling financially secure and 14.67 per cent did not feel that the family needs were being satisfied within the total family income. These women felt that taking a job would solve their problem. Thus, it can be said that a number of unemployed women may be motivated to take a job for financial security and enhancement of family income. In fact, 13.33 per cent the MUE group has clearly stated money to be the motivating factor for wanting to take a job (Table 4.100).

However, 89.33 per cent of MUE women report feeling financially secure and 85.33 per cent report finding that the family income is sufficient. This conveys the idea that most of these women are fairly satisfied within their socio-economic set-up.

Table 4.97 : Feel Financially Secure

Groups	Yes	No	Total	χ^2	p
ME	73 (97.33%)	2 (2.67%)	75		
MUE	67 (89.33%)	8 (10.66%)	75	10.89	0.01
SE	75 (100%)	0 (0%)	75		

Table 4.98 : Total Family Income Adequate for Family Needs

Groups	Yes	No	Total	χ^2	p
ME	74 (98.67%)	1 (1.33%)	75		
MUE	64 (85.33%)	11 (14.67%)	75	19.55	0.01
SE	75 (100%)	0 (0%)	75		

Table 4.99 : Desire to take a Job

Group	Yes	No	Total
MUE	62 (82.67%)	13 (17.33%)	75

Table 4.100 : Reasons for wanting to take a Job

Reasons	Number	Percentage
For Independence	12	16
To Reduce Boredom	20	26.67
To Pass Time	10	13.33
For Financial Reasons	10	13.33
Others (High qualification, self fulfilment, presently having free time)	10	13.33
Total	62	82.67

Table 4.101 : Reasons for not wanting to take a Job

Reasons	Number	Percentage
Do not feel like working	4	5.33
Children are small	4	5.33
No Response	5	6.67
Total	13	17.33

Discussion

An overall view of the results tends to lend greater support to the socialization hypothesis than the social structural hypothesis. Women of all the three groups are quite similar to each other on a number of need related aspects like Affiliation, Nurturance, Deference, Order, Intraception.

All these aspects are related to the prevalent sex-role expectations from women who are required to play a major role within the family system. Presence of these characteristics would be desirable for an adequate functioning within the family roles of women. Hence, it may be concluded that these are some of the basic characteristics which would be instilled within the women during the process of socialization, so that they may be able to play their adult social roles more efficiently.

However, there are some characteristics which appear to be specific to the housewife and some to career roles.

The married employed women are identical to married unemployed and distinct from single employed women on some other needs like *n*-Autonomy, *n*-Dominance and *n*-Aggression.

These needs are strongly associated with the role of the housewife which they are playing at present. On the other hand the married employed and single employed appear to be more similar and different from married unemployed on some of the work related needs like Achievement, Succourance and Exhibition.

A look into the social background of these women shows that the parents of married unemployed women had more often planned for marriage only for their daughters but not so for the married employed whose parents had planned for both marriage and career. The parents of single employed had given more importance to career. The parents of the career women had also motivated their daughters to prepare for taking an employment. These differences in the rearing atmosphere may account for the fact that married employed women are similar to married unemployed on housewife role related aspects on one hand and to single employed on career role related aspects. It is likely that their parents would have reared them in such a way that they may develop a combination of characteristics suitable for both the roles.

Another aspect of socialization hypothesis which is confirmed by the results is that when family and career roles appear in opposition adjustments are made in favour of the family roles. The married employed have directed their achievement orientation towards academic activities in contrast to administrative and they are more ready to leave the job if family conditions require it. They given highest priority to the family despite being in job but the single women who are free to these constraints have shown greater orientation towards power related administrative aspects of job and they do not feel pulled by home or family responsibilities.

Despite the home *vs.* job related conflicts the employed women enjoy the positive, social, economic consequences of their employed status. Both the employed groups have been found to have higher self-esteem than the married unemployed women.

It has also been observed in the results that women who have characteristics not in consonance with their present role, suffer a loss of self-esteem married employed women who have more feminine characteristic in fact have a higher self-esteem, on the other hand unemployed women who have higher need for achievement also have lower self-esteem. The single employed women who have lower need achievement and have higher need for affiliation and *n*-Nurturance also have lower self-esteem. It would then appear that the early socialization has a greater impact than the present social structures.

In the total situations the married employed women emerge to be in the strongest position and the married unemployed in the weakest. In this state of social flux where a new order is emerging, the role of the housewife alone is somewhat devalued. Women who are receiving higher levels of education are expected to share the load of the family finances to become more self-sufficient and accomplish something more than just household tasks. The older traditional pattern of rearing the female child, hence, needs to undergo a change so that the women of tomorrow are geared to take wider range of responsibilities and become pioneers in newer fields. But all this must not be accomplished at the cost of breaking the family system. The importance of the family and movement outside the home has to be balanced in such a fashion by the women of the years to come that they are able to keep the family system intact and yet be able to touch new horizons.

5

Résumé

The modern educated urban women is gradually entering areas of activities and roles which are usually considered to be masculine. It is important to understand how the women operate within these changing roles. The present investigation, hence, was planned to make a comparative study of the Need patterns and Self-Esteem of Married Employed, Married Unemployed and Single Employed women. On the basis of the review of literature and the theoretical bases available, certain hypotheses were formulated.

It was expected that the married employed women who share the housewife role with the married unemployed women are likely to be similar to them and different from Single Employed Women on needs like Orderliness, Affiliation, Nurturance, Intraception, Deference, Abasement, Succourance, and Heterosexuality.

On the other hand the Married Employed share the worker role with the Single Employed women and, hence, are likely to be similar to them and different from Married Unemployed women on needs like Achievement, Exhibition, Autonomy, Dominance, Change, Endurance and Aggression. Both the employed groups were also expected to have higher Self-Esteem.

A sample consisting of 75 Married Employed, 75 Single Employed and 75 Married Unemployed matching in educational and socio-economic background was chosen from universities of Varanasi.

TPPS was used to assess their need patterns. The scale uses

forced choice format of items and measures 15 need related aspects *viz.*

n-Achievement, *n*-Deference,
n-Order, *n*-Exhibition,
n-Autonomy, *n*-Affiliation,
n-Intraception, *n*-Succourance,
n-Dominance, *n*-Abasement,
n-Nurturance, *n*-Change,
n-Endurance, *n*-Heterosexuality,
n-Aggression.

Indian adaptation of Rosenberg's Self-Esteem scale was used to measure Self-Esteem. An Interview Schedule prepared by the author was used to elicit information related to certain socio-cultural aspects like Parental Influences, Role of Family, Attitude towards Career, Home *vs.* Job Conflict, Views regarding job relating aspects.

The tests were administered on the sample individually and the data thus collected was analyzed using Mean, S.D, One-way ANOVA, '*t*' test and χ^2 test.

The results have been examined in the light of socialization hypothesis and structural hypothesis. The socialization hypothesis predicts that Married Employed Women and Married Unemployed Women will be quite similar whereas according to structural hypothesis Married Employed and Single Employed should be more similar.

In fact our results are more in consonance with the socialization hypothesis. Considering the fact that the three groups did not differ in any significant measure on a number of needs basically related with the female sex-role identity like Deference, Affiliation, Intraception and Nurturance. They may as well as be taken as typical femininity indicators bordering on generality.

However, differences regarding the need patterns and levels of self-esteem between employed and unemployed women have also been found. Employed women, single or married are more achievement oriented and less succourant than unemployed women. They also appear to be having higher self-esteem than the married unemployed. The prevalent Indian social structure, in fact, reinforces the development of succourant behaviour in women. However, women entering the worker role have been found to be less succourant and more achievement oriented. It is likely that they are reared in such a way by their parents that they seek employment as a means to remain independent.

Further their high *n*-Achievement would suggest that their pursuits for success may also be heightened and get channelized in the same direction as is usually defined.

The need-patterns and self-esteem of high scorers and low scorers on *n*-Achievement within each role was also examined and compared. The MUE women with high scores on *n*-Achievement were highest on *n*-Exhibition, *n*-Dominance, *n*-Change and lowest on *n*-Endurance and Self-esteem. These results would suggest that MUE women with high need achievement do possess certain needs which may be better satisfied in an employed role than their present role. Their low self-esteem may probably be reflecting their sense of incompatibility with their present role.

The interesting aspect in context to low scorers on *n*-Achievement is that the SE group is highest on *n*-Affiliation and *n*-Nurturance. Both the needs are such that the chances of their fulfilment are lower in their present role. The single women with low *n*-Achievement have lower self-esteem as compared to the ME, whereas the SE women with high need achievement were found to have higher self-esteem.

The results related to high and low scorers on *n*-Achievement indicate that being in roles which do not permit satisfaction of certain needs which one possesses may have a negative effect on the psychological well-being of the person and further it also appears that the employment factor as such may not be directly related to psychological well-being as is usually supposed, but the need pattern may be playing a mediating role.

The comparison of high Self-esteem and low Self-esteem women had indicated that HS Est ME were lower on *n*-Achievement and higher on *n*-Abasement as compared to SE. However, in the total sample comparison no differences had existed on these needs between MUE and SE. Furthermore, HS Est ME were higher on *n*-Deference and lower on *n*-Exhibition and *n*-Dominance than MUE. However, in the total group score no differences had existed between ME and MUE on *n*-Deference and *n*-Dominance.

HS Est ME would appear to be less achievement oriented, less exhibitionistic, more deferent, less dominant and higher on *n*-Abasement.

Thus, despite being in non-traditional role, the ME women are more in consonance with their sex-role identity and thereby probably getting social acceptance and maintaining a high Self-esteem. The Married Unemployed women on the other hand may be increasing their self-esteem through dominant and exhibitionistic behaviour. The SE group may seek to maintain their self-esteem through fulfilment of high need achievement. The predominance of sex-role identity can be observed here again.

The results analysed and discussed above provide indications that sex-role identity may be the prominent feature governing the behaviour of women within either traditional or non-traditional roles. The differences that do exist between employed and unemployed women may be there due to differences in early socialization pattern itself.

In the light of the above discussion it was considered meaningful to examine whether there were any differences or similarities in the rearing patterns and the socio-cultural conditions of the three comparison groups.

The fathers of both the employed groups as compared to unemployed group were found to be higher in educational level, had motivated their daughters to seek employment had given equal importance to both marriage and career for their daughters' future and mostly held positive attitudes about working women. However, such differences were not found in the context of the mothers of these women.

It was also found that the employed married women are surrounded by relatives who are positively happy about their work role but people around the unemployed women do not convey this positive feeling even though they may not be negative either regarding their present housewife status.

MUE were found to receive more support and help as compared to ME. So, it is natural that significantly more of MUE have reported being satisfied with the help and support received than ME. It may be remembered here that MUE were found to be significantly more succourant than ME.

Significantly more of the married employed subjects had reported that they were striving for academic success whereas the SE have reported to be striving more for administrative success. The SE had also been found to be higher on needs like autonomy and dominance which are likely to be satisfied by achieving administrative success.

More of the ME women appear to be facing conflict between job and home responsibilities as compared to single employed.

Married Employed women thus appear to be striking a balance between the two roles *i.e.* one of the housewife and the other of the worker. She may be facing related tensions but she is able to maintain the balance and enjoys the facilitating effects of the employment as well as the social and familial support from her home maker role. Any conflict between the two roles does not seem to have any deleterious effect on her adjustment as a whole.

Suggestions for Further Research

Every investigation is planned with an intention to study a problem thoroughly, from every aspect, but despite this certain aspects may be overlooked inadvertently. Sometimes, during the process of investigation certain lacunas are discovered. These omissions and lacunas create the background for further research.

It was felt during the analysis that the study, if replicated on a much larger sample, may yield more meaningful results specially in context to comparison of women with High and Low need for Achievement and High and Low Self-Esteem. Even with the small sample the analysis has revealed certain interesting observations.

Another suggested line of investigation is to explore the personality of women who are more pioneering like business women, engineers etc. The present study was conducted on women in teaching profession. It is generally considered that the teachers role is not to in consonant with the prevalent concepts of sex-role identity.

In the present study, self-acceptance aspect of Self-Esteem was studied. It may be more meaningful if other aspects of Self-Esteem like self-confidence alongwith some other measures of psychological well-being are also studied.

APPENDIX - I

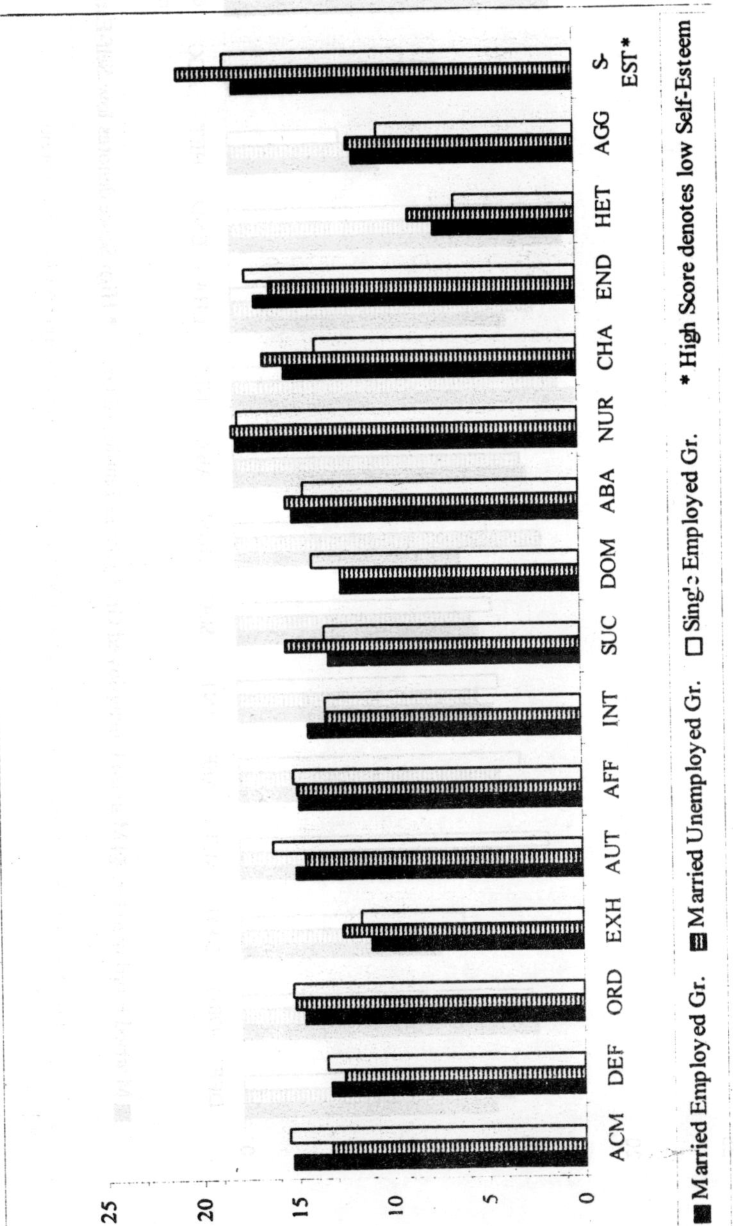

Fig. 1 : Mean Scores on Need Variables and Self-Esteem for ME, MUE and SE Groups

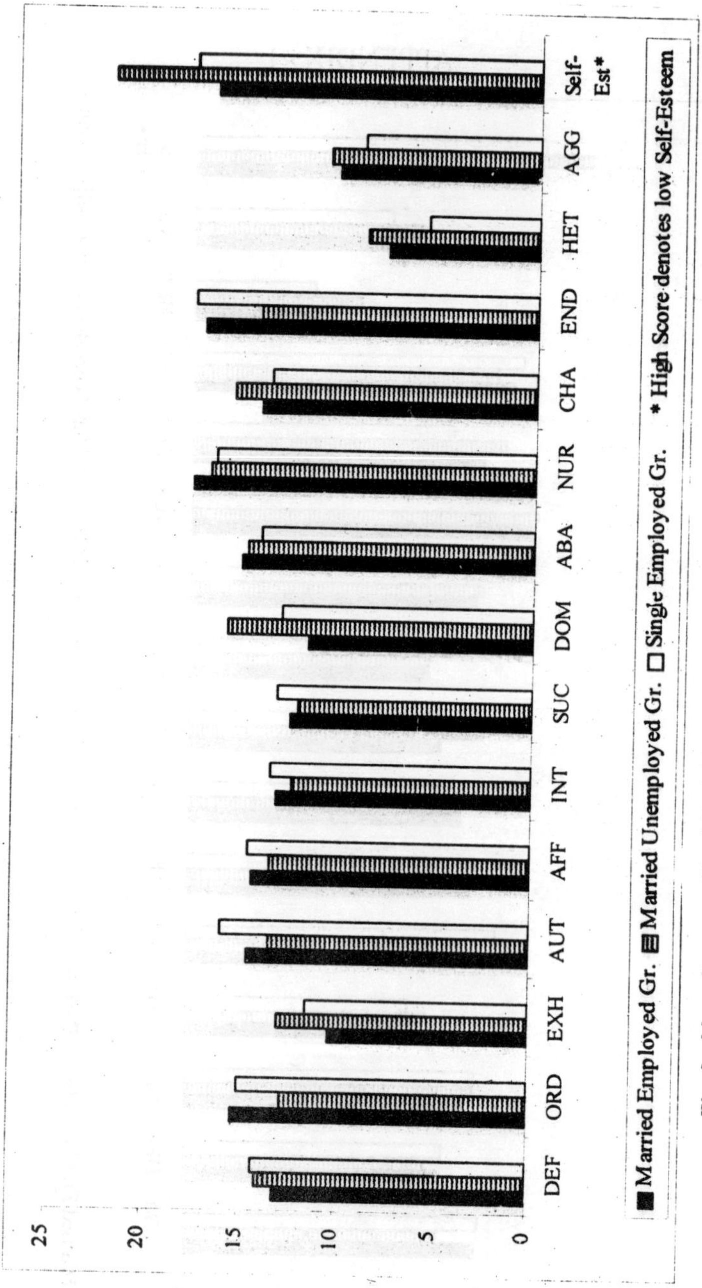

Fig. 2 : Mean Scores on Need Variables and Self-Esteem for High Scorers on *n*-Achievement

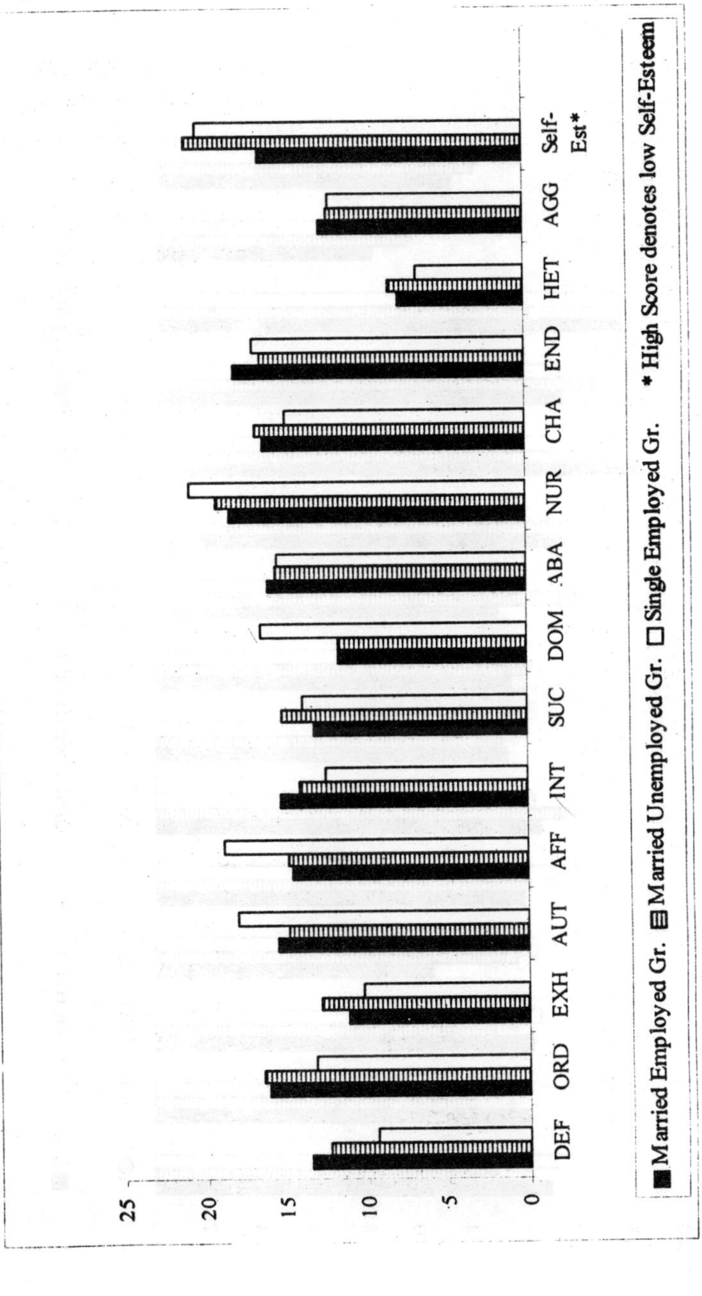

Fig. 3 : Mean Scores on Need Variables and Self-Esteem for Low Scorers on *n*-Achievement

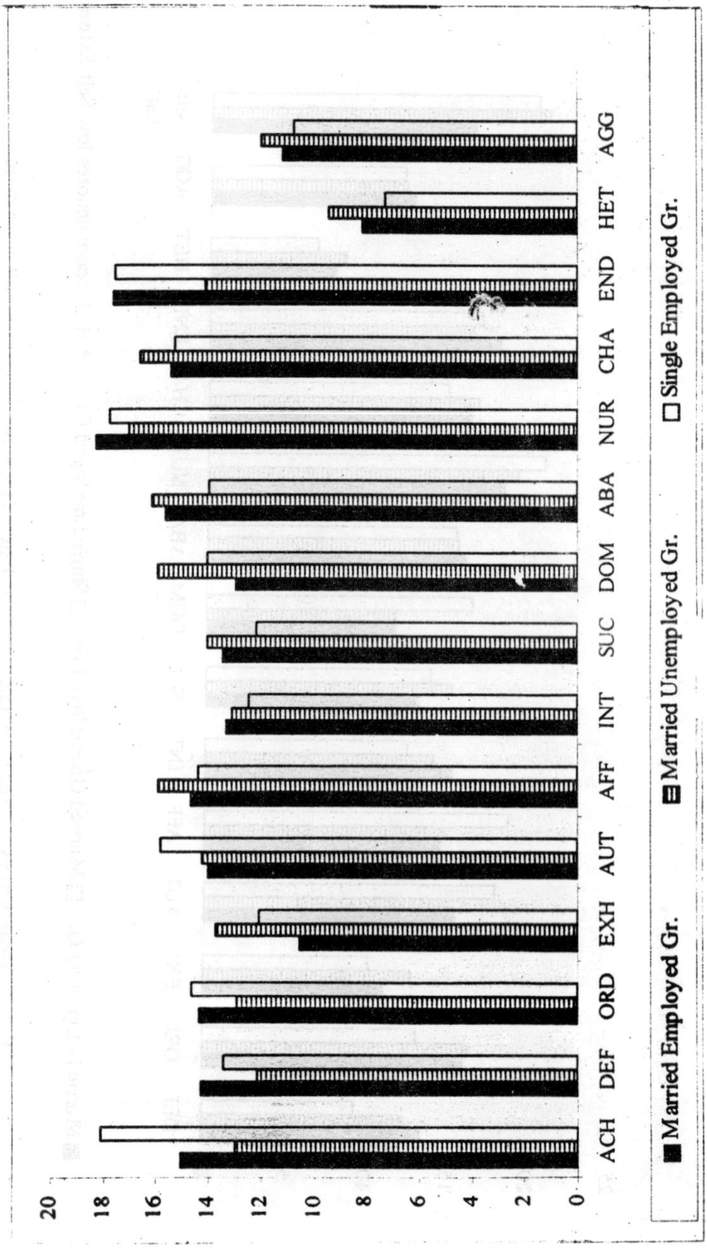

Fig. 4 : Mean Scores on Need Variables for High Self-Esteem Subjects

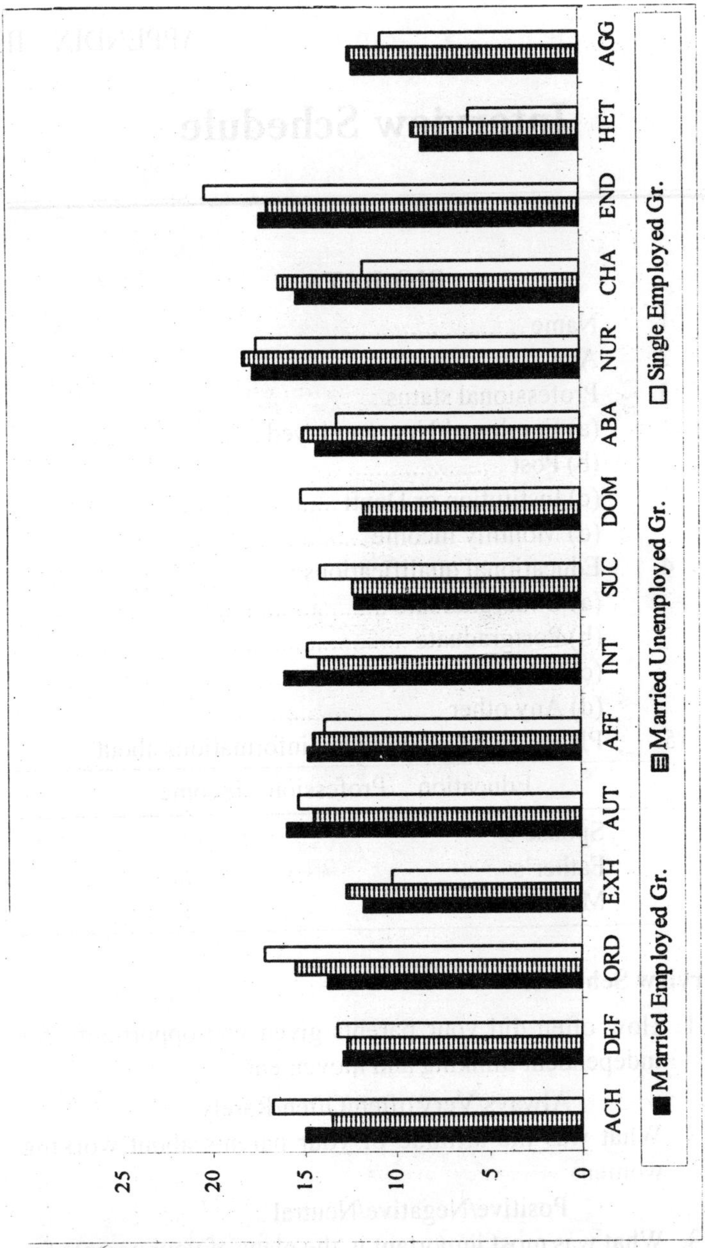

Fig. 5 :Mean Scores on Need Variables for Low Self-Esteem Subjects

APPENDIX - II

Interview Schedule

BIO-DATA

1. Name ....
2. Age ....
3. Professional status :
   (a) Employed/Non-employed ....
   (b) Post ....
   (c) Institution or Deptt ....
   (d) Monthly income ....
4. Educational qualifications :
   (a) Undergraduate ....
   (b) Postgraduate ....
   (c) Doctorate ....
   (d) Any other ....
5. Please give the following informations about :

	Education	Profession	Income
Spouse's			
Father's			
Mother's			

Interview Schedule

1. How often did your parents given you opportunity for independent thinking and movement :

   Always/Very often/Often/Rarely
2. What was the attitude of your parents about working women:

   Positive/Negative/Neutral
3. What was most important in the plans of your parents for

your future :

(a) Career (b) Marriage

(c) Both equally (d) Any other

4. What do your immediate family members feel about your
   (a) Being a career woman (for employed woman)
   (b) Not being a career woman (for non-employed woman)

	Extremely satisfied	Satisfied	Neutral	Dissatisfied	Extremely dissatisfied
Husband					
Children					
In-laws					
Other relatives					

5. What kind of help and support do you receive from persons listed below :

	Household work	Children's care	Outside responsibilities
Parents			
In-laws			
Husband			
Children			
Servants			
Others			

6. Do you feel satisfied with the amount of help and support received?

   Yes/No

7. Do you feel that a career woman commands more respect than housewife?

   Yes/No

8. Do you feel that a career woman is less satisfied and less happier than a housewife?

   Yes/No

9. Do you feel that a woman should concentrate more on her home than her career?

   Yes/No

10. Do you feel financially secure?

Yes/No

11. Do you feel that all your and your family's needs are being satisfied within the total family income?

Yes/No

If not then what steps do you think are necessary to supplement income?

(For Employed Women only)

12. Who motivated you to take the job?
No one/Parents/Husband/In-laws/Friends/Relatives/Children/Any other
13. Do you ever think that because of home responsibilities you are unable to attend to your job properly?
Always/Very often/Often/Rarely
14. Do you ever think that because of a job you are unable to attend to your home properly?
Always/Very often/Often/Rarely
15. What is your highest professional ambition? ...
16. In your job which aspects do you think are more important:
(1) Academic
(2) Administrative
(3) Both equally
17. What do you strive for in your job?
(1) Academic
(2) Administrative
(3) Any other
18. What were your reasons for taking the job? ...
19. Would you like to leave your job, if conditions permit?
Yes/No
20. Are you satisfied with your job?
Yes/No
Give reasons ....
21. Do your colleagues regard and respect you for being a career woman:
(a) Male colleagues Yes/No
(b) Female colleagues Yes/No
22. What are the disadvantages and advantages in being a working person?

(a) Male colleagues Yes/No
(b) Female colleagues Yes/No

22. What are the disadvantages and advantages in being a working person?

    ....

    (For Unemployed Women only)

23. Do you wish to take a job?

    Yes/No

    Give reasons for your answers ....

24. Does any one in your family motivate you to take a job?

    Yes/No

    If yes, who ....

APPENDIX - III

The Rosenberg's Self-Esteem Questionnaire

(Hindi Version)

निर्देश

इस प्रश्नावली में कुछ कथन दिए गए हैं जिसे आप ध्यानपूर्वक पढ़िए। प्रत्येक कथन के निम्न सम्भावित उत्तरों में से आपको अपने लिए जो सही लगे उसे घेरकर अपनी सहमति दें। उदाहरण के लिए :–

मैं वर्ग का सबसे अच्छा छात्र हूँ।

पूर्णतः सहमत	सहमत	असहमत	पूर्णतः असहमत
×	⊗	×	×

अगर आप इस कथन से सहमत हैं तो इस प्रकार घेरा बनाकर अपनी अभिव्यक्ति दीजिए। सभी प्रश्नों के उत्तर देना आवश्यक है। आपके उत्तर पूर्णरूप से गोपनीय रखे जाएँगे।

	पूर्णतः सहमत	सहमत	असहमत	पूर्णतः असहमत
1. मैं अनुभव करती हूँ/करता हूँ कि मैं भी उतनी ही योग्य हूँ/उतना ही योग्य हूँ जितने कि दूसरे लोग	×	×	×	×
2. मैं अनुभव करती हूँ कि/करता हूँ कि मुझमें बहुत सारे अच्छे गुण हैं	×	×	×	×
3. प्रत्येक दृष्टिकोण से मैं यह सोचने के लिए बाध्य हूँ कि मैं एक असफल व्यक्ति हूँ	×	×	×	×

4. मैं भी वह सब कर सकती हूँ/कर सकता हूँ जो दूसरे लोग कर सकते हैं	×	×	×	×
5. मैं अनुभव करती हूँ/करता हूँ कि मेरे अन्दर गर्व करने लायक कुछ नहीं है	×	×	×	×
6. मैं अपने प्रति स्वीकारात्मक मनोवृत्ति रखती/रखता हूँ	×	×	×	×
7. मैं अपने पूर्णतः सन्तुष्ट हूँ	×	×	×	×
8. काश! मुझमें और आत्म सम्मान होता	×	×	×	×
9. कभी-कभी मैं अपने आपको बेकार महसूस करती/करता हूँ	×	×	×	×
10. कभी-कभी मैं सोचती/सोचता हूँ कि मैं बिल्कुल अच्छी/अच्छा नहीं हूँ	×	×	×	×

APPENDIX - IV

Tripathi Personal Preference Schedule

आप की पसन्द : एक अनुसूची

(महिलाएँ)

निर्देश

इस अनुसूची में दो-दो वाक्यों के बहुत से जोड़े क्रम से दिए हुए हैं। प्रत्येक जोड़े के दोनों वाक्यों में ऐसी बाते हैं जिन्हें या तो आप करना पसन्द करती हैं या जिन्हें करने को आपका जी चाहता है। कुछ वाक्यों में ऐसे भाव या अनुभूतियाँ हैं जिन्हें आप महसूस या अनुभव करती हैं। प्रत्येक जोड़े के दोनों वाक्यों को ध्यान से पढ़कर आपको यह तय करना है इन वाक्यों में कही गई दोनों बातों में से कौन-सी आपके पसन्द की है या आपके बारे में ठीक-ठीक लागू होती है। अगर दोनों ही बातें आपको पसन्द हैं तो यह देखिए कि दोनों में से कौन-सी अधिक पसन्द है। उसे आप चुन लीजिए और जो कम पसन्द हो या नापसन्द हो उसे छोड़ दीजिए। एक उदाहरण लीजिए :

(क) मैं घर के बाहर कायदे के कपड़ों में निकलना पसन्द करती हूँ।

(ख) मैं अपने उद्देश्य की पूर्ति के लिए सही तरीकों का इस्तेमाल पसन्द करती हूँ।

ऊपर के दोनों वाक्यों में दो बातें हैं : 1. 'घर के बाहर कायदे के कपड़ों में निकलना'; 2. 'अपने उद्देश्य की पूर्ति के लिए सही तरीकों का इस्तेमाल करना'।

अब देखिए कि इन दोनों में से कौन-सी बात आपके पसन्द की है या आपकी पसन्द के अधिक करीब है–उसे आप चुन लीजिए और दूसरी को छोड़ दीजिए।

ठीक इसी तरह आप अनुभूति वाले वाक्यों को लें। इनमें भी आपकी अनुभूति के अधिक नजदीक जो वाक्य हो उसे चुन लें।

ध्यान रखें कि आप किसी वाक्य को यह सोचकर न चुनें कि आपको 'क्या पसन्द करना चाहिए' और 'कैसा महसूस करना चाहिए', बल्कि यह सोचकर चुनें कि आप सचमुच क्या पसन्द करती हैं, कैसा महसूस करती हैं। यानी दोनों बातों में से कौन-सी बात आपके बारे मे ठीक-ठाक लागू होती है।

यह कोई परीक्षा नहीं है। इसलिए आपके जवाब के सही या गलत होने की कोई बात नहीं है। केवल आपको अपनी पसन्द की बात वाले वाक्य को चुन लेना है।

अगर ऐसा हो कि किसी जोड़े की दोनों ही बातें आपको नापसन्द हैं तो यह देखिए कि कौन-सी बात आपको कम नापसन्द है उसी को चुन लीजिए।

हाँ, हर जोड़ें में से एक वाक्य अवश्य चुनिए। कोई जोड़ा छूटने न पाए।

वाक्यों के हर जोड़े को ध्यान से पढ़िए, विचार कीजिए और अपनी पसन्द की बात वाले वाक्य को चुन लीजिए।

इस पुस्तिका पर कुछ न लिखिए। आपको एक उत्तर-पत्र (answer-sheet) अलग से दिया गया है जिसमें वाक्यों के जोड़ों की क्रम-संख्या दी गई है और प्रत्येक क्रम-संख्या के सामने 'क' और 'ख' दिए हुए हैं। इस अनुसूची के वाक्यों के जोड़े की क्रम-संख्या और उत्तर-पत्र के जोड़े की क्रम-संख्या को ठीक से मिलाइए, और तब 'क' तथा 'ख' में से जिसे आपने चुना है, उत्तर-पत्र में उसी को ('क' या 'ख' को) गोल निशान से घेर दीजिए। उदाहरण नीचे दिया गया है :

८ (क)
ख

९ क
(ख)

यहाँ नम्बर 8 में 'क' और 9 में 'ख' को चुना गया है, अतः उन्हें घेर दिया गया है। इसी तरह आपको भी अपने उत्तर-पत्र में निशान बनाना है।

1. (क) मैं मित्रों के दुख-दर्द में शरीक होना पसन्द करती हूँ।
   (ख) मैं जो भी काम हाथ में लेती हूँ उसे सफलतापूर्वक पूरा करना पसन्द करती हूँ।
2. (क) महान् पुरुषों की जीवनियाँ पढ़ना मुझे अच्छा लगता है।
   (ख) मैं चाहती हूँ कि मैं कोई ऐसा काम करूँ जिसका बड़ा महत्त्व हो।
3. (क) मैं कोई मुश्किल काम शुरू करने के पहले उसकी एक योजना बना लेना पसन्द करती हूँ।

(ख) मैं जो भी काम हाथ में लेती हूँ उसे सफलतापूर्वक पूरा करना पसन्द करती हूँ।

4. (क) दोस्तों की मण्डली में मनोरंजक चुटकुले और किस्से सुनाना मुझे अच्छा लगता है।

(ख) मैं ऐसी पहेलियाँ और समस्याएँ हल करना पसन्द करती हूँ जो दूसरों के लिए मुश्किल पड़ती हैं।

5. (क) मैं यह चाहती हूँ कि मुझे जो कुछ करना है उसका फैसला बिना किसी दूसरे की मदद के खुद करूँ।

(ख) मैं चाहती हूँ कि मैं कोई बड़ी किताब लिख सकती।

6. (क) मैं जिस काम मे हाथ लगाती हूँ उसे खूब अच्छी तरह करना पसन्द करती हूँ।

(ख) मैं यह जानना चाहती हूँ कि जिन बातों में मेरी दिलचस्पी है उनके बारे में महान् व्यक्तियों के क्या विचार हैं।

7. (क) मुझे नए-नए लोगों से मिलना-जुलना अच्छा लगता है।

(ख) मैं रीति-रिवाज के अनुकूल रहना पसन्द करती हूँ और ऐसा कुछ नहीं करना चाहती जिसे आदरणीय जन परम्परा-विरुद्ध समझते हैं।

8. (क) कोई काम शुरू करने के पहले मैं उसके हर पहलू को सोच-समझ लेना पसन्द करती हूँ।

(ख) मैं यह जानना चाहती हूँ कि जिन बातों में मेरी दिलचस्पी है उनके बारे में महान् व्यक्तियों के क्या विचार हैं।

9. (क) मैं ऐसी बातें करना पसन्द करती हूँ जिन्हें लोग सूझ-बूझ और दिलचस्प समझें।

(ख) मैं जिन लोगों की कद्र करती हूँ उन्हे अपना नेता मानना मुझे पसन्द है।

10. (क) बिना इस बात की परवाह किए हुए कि दूसरे क्या सोचेंगे, मैं अपने ढंग से काम करना पसन्द करती हूँ।

(ख) अपने समूह का कार्यक्रम दूसरे सदस्यों द्वारा तय किया जाना मुझे पसन्द है।

11. (क) मैं जिस काम में हाथ लगाती हूँ उसे खूब अच्छी तरह करना पसन्द करती हूँ।

(ख) कोई काम शुरू करने के पहले मैं उसके हर पहलू को सोच-समझ लेना पसन्द करती हूँ।

12. (क) अपने से श्रेष्ठ लोग जब किसी काम को अच्छे ढंग से करते हैं तो उनकी तारीफ करने को जी चाहता है।
    (ख) यदि मुझे कहीं बाहर जाना हो तो मैं उसकी पूरी तैयारी पहले से ही कर लेना पसन्द करती हूँ।
13. (क) मैं किसी समस्या या पहेली में उस समय तक लगे रहना पसन्द करती हूँ जब तक कि वह हल न हो जाए।
    (ख) मैं अपनी चिट्ठियाँ और दूसरे कागज-पत्र कायदे से अलग-अलग फाइल बनाकर रखना पसन्द करती हूँ।
14. (क) समूह में मैं यह चाहती हूँ कि सब लोग मेरी ही ओर ध्यान दें।
    (ख) मुझे किस समय क्या खाना चाहिए यह निश्चित रखना तथा नित्य ठीक समय से खा लेना पसन्द है।
15. (क) बिना इस बात की परवाह किए हुए कि दूसरे क्या सोचेंगे, मैं अपने ढंग से काम करना पसन्द करती हूँ।
    (ख) मैं अपना जीवन-क्रम इस तरह व्यवस्थित कर लेना चाहती हूँ जो बिना किसी खास हेर-फेर के आसानी से चलता रहे।
16. (क) मैं यह चाहती हूँ कि मुझे किसी व्यवसाय, कार्य या विशेष ज्ञान के क्षेत्र में विशेषज्ञ माना जाए।
    (ख) मैं ऐसी बातें करना पसन्द करती हूँ जिनहें लोग सूझ-बूझ की और दिलचस्प समझें।
17. (क) मैं आदेशों का पालन करना तथा जिस बात की मुझसे उम्मीद की जाती हो उसे पूरा करना पसन्द करती हूँ।
    (ख) दोस्तों की मण्डली में मनोरंजक किस्से और चुटकुले सुनाना मुझे अच्छा लगता है।
18. (क) मैं अपना जीवन-क्रम इस तरह व्यवस्थित कर लेना पसन्द करती हूँ जो बिना किसी खास हेर-फेर के आसानी से चलता रहे।
    (ख) समूह में मैं यह चाहती हूँ कि सब लोग मेरी ही ओर ध्यान दें।
19. (क) मैं ऐसी बहस या बातचीत में भाग लेना पसन्द करती हूँ जिसका विषय काम-वृत्ति (सेक्स) हो।
    (ख) मैं ऐसे शब्दों का प्रयोग करना पसन्द करती हूँ जिनका अर्थ लोग अक्सर नहीं जानते।
20. (क) किसी विषय में मैं जो कुछ महसूस करती हूँ उसे कह देना पसन्द करती हूँ।

(ख) मैं जान-बूझ कर ऐसे प्रश्न पूछना पसन्द करती हूँ जिनका जवाब कोई न दे सके।

21. (क) मैं यह चाहती हूँ कि मुझे किसी व्यवसाय, कार्य या विशेष ज्ञान के क्षेत्र में विशेषज्ञ माना जाए।

(ख) मुझे जो कुछ करना है उसके करने में मैं आजादी महसूस करना चाहती हूँ।

22. (क) कोई योजना बनाते समय मैं उन लोगों से सुझाव लेना पसन्द करती हूँ जिनके विचारों का मैं आदर करती हूँ।

(ख) मुझे जो कुछ करना है उसके करने में मैं आजादी महसूस करना चाहती हूँ।

23. (क) मैं अपनी काम करने की जगह या मेज पर सब चीजें ढंग से सजाकर रखना पसन्द करती हूँ।

(ख) मैं यह चाहती हूँ कि मुझे जो कुछ करना है उसका फैसला बिना किसी दूसरे की मदद के खुद करूँ।

24. (क) दूसरों के सामने मैं अपनी बहादुरी और अपने जीवन की आश्चर्यजनक बातों की दास्तान सुनाना पसन्द करती हूँ।

(ख) मैं जिम्मेदारियों और बन्धनों से दूर रहना पसन्द करती हूँ।

25. (क) मैं कभी-कभी इतना गुस्से में आ जाती हूँ कि चीजों को उठा-पटक और तोड़-फोड़ देने को जी चाहता है।

(ख) मुझे ऐसे काम करना पसन्द है जिन्हें रीति-रिवाज के विरुद्ध समझा जाता है।

26. (क) मैं चाहती हूँ कि मैं कोई ऐसा काम करूँ जिसका बड़ा महत्त्व हो।

(ख) मुझे अपने मित्रों के काम आना अच्छा लगता है।

27. (क) मैं आदेशों का पालन करना तथा जिस बात की मुझसे उम्मीद की जाती हो उसे पूरा करना पसन्द करती हूँ।

(ख) मैं अपने मित्रों से घनिष्ठ सम्बन्ध रखना पसन्द करती हूँ।

28. (क) मैं कोई मुश्किल काम शुरू करने के पहले उसकी एक योजना बना लेना पसन्द करती हूँ।

(ख) मैं ऐसी मण्डली में रहना पसन्द करती हूँ जहाँ आपस में मैत्रीभाव तथा स्नेह रहे।

29. (क) कभी-कभी मैं कोई काम सिर्फ यह देखने के लिए करना पसन्द करती

हूँ कि उसका दूसरों पर क्या असर होता है।

(ख) मैं अपनी सभी बातों में मित्रों को शामिल रखना पसन्द करती हूँ।

30. (क) मुझे जो कुछ करना है उसके करने में मैं आजादी महसूस करना चाहती हूँ।

(ख) अपने मित्रों को चिट्ठियाँ लिखना मुझे अच्छा लगता है।

31. (क) मैं चाहती हूँ कि मैं कोई बड़ी किताब लिख सकती।

(ख) मैं अपने को दूसरों की परिस्थिति में रखकर यह समझना चाहती हूँ कि उस स्थिति में मुझे कैसा लगता है।

32. (क) मैं रीति-रिवाज के अनुकूल रहना पसन्द करती हूँ और ऐसा कुछ नहीं करना चाहती जिसे आदरणीय जन परम्परा-विरुद्ध समझते हैं।

(ख) मैं अपने मित्रों के व्यक्तित्व पर विचार करना और यह समझने की कोशिश करना पसन्द करती हूँ कि वे जैसे भी हैं इसका कारण क्या है।

33. (क) मैं अपनी चिट्ठियाँ और दूसरे कागज-पत्र कायदे से अलग-अलग फाइल बनाकर रखना पसन्द करती हूँ।

(ख) मैं अपने को दूसरों की परिस्थिति में रखकर यह समझना चाहती हूँ कि उस स्थिति में मुझे कैसा लगता है।

34. (क) मैं अपनी सफलताओं के बारे में बातें करना पसन्द करती हूँ।

(ख) मैं दूसरों के व्यवहारों का अध्ययन और विश्लेषण करना पसन्द करती हूँ।

35. (क) मैं ऐसे मौकों से बचना चाहती हूँ जहाँ मुझसे रीति-रिवाज निभाने की आशा की जाए।

(ख) मैं दूसरों की अनुभूतियों और इच्छाओं की छान-बीन करना पसन्द करती हूँ।

36. (क) मैं ऐसी पहेलियाँ और समस्याएँ हल करना पसन्द करती हूँ जो दूसरों के लिए मुश्किल पड़ती हैं।

(ख) मैं चाहती हूँ कि मेरे मित्र मुझसे अधिक-से-अधिक स्नेह रखें।

37. (क) कोई योजना बनाते समय मैं उन लोगों से सुझाव लेना पसन्द करती हूँ जिनके विचारों का मैं आदर करती हूँ।

(ख) मैं चाहती हूँ कि मेरे मित्र मुझसे सहृदयता का बर्ताव करें।

38. (क) किसी काम को शुरू करने के पहले उसकी योजना बना लेना और उसकी तैयारी कर लेना मुझे पसन्द है।

(ख) किसी काम में असफल होने पर मैं चाहती हूँ कि मेरे मित्र मुझे प्रोत्साहित करें।

39. (क) दूसरों के बीच होने पर मैं ऐसी वेशभूषा रखना चाहती हूँ कि लोगों की निगाहें मेरी ओर उठें और लोग उस पर अपनी राय दें।

(ख) जब मैं बीमार होती हूँ तो चाहती हूँ कि मेरे मित्र मेरे लिए दुखी हों।

40. (क) मैं अधिकारी-वर्ग के लोगों की आलोचना करना पसन्द करती हूँ।

(ख) मैं चाहती हूँ कि मेरे मित्र मेरे छोटे-मोटे काम खुशी-खुशी कर दिया करें।

41. (क) मैं ऐसी पहेलियाँ और समस्याएँ हल करना पसन्द करती हूँ जो दूसरों के लिए मुश्किल पड़ती हैं।

(ख) मैं लोगों को यह बताना चाहती हूँ कि उन्हें अपना काम किस ढंग से करना चाहिए।

42. (क) मैं रीति-रिवाज के अनुकूल रहना पसन्द करती हूँ और ऐसा कुछ नहीं करना चाहती जिसे आदरणीय जन परम्परा-विरुद्ध समझते हैं।

(ख) अवसर मिलने पर मैं दूसरों के कामों की देख-रेख करना तथा उन्हें आदेश देना पसन्द करती हूँ।

43. (क) मैं अपनी काम की जगह या मेज पर सब चीजें ढंग से सजाकर रखना पसन्द करती हूँ।

(ख) किसी समिति में काम करने पर मैं चाहती हूँ कि मुझे उसका अध्यक्ष बनाया जाए।

44. (क) दूसरों के सामने मैं अपनी बहादुरी और अपने जीवन की आश्चर्यजनक बातों की दास्तान सुनाना पसन्द करती हूँ।

(ख) मैं जो चाहती हूँ वही करने के लिए दूसरों को समझा-बुझाकर राजी करना और उन पर अपना प्रभाव डालना पसन्द करती हूँ।

45. (क) मुझे ऐसे काम करना पसन्द है जिन्हें रीति-रिवाज के विरुद्ध समझा जाता है।

(ख) मेरी इच्छा रहती है कि दूसरे लोग मुझे अपना नेता मानें।

46. (क) मैं यह चाहती हूँ कि मुझे किसी व्यवसाय, कार्य या विशेष ज्ञान के क्षेत्र में विशेषज्ञ माना जाए।

(ख) अगर मुझसे कोई गलती हो जाती है तो मैं यह महसूस करती हूँ कि मुझे इसकी सजा भुगतनी चाहिए।

47. (क) कोई योजना बनाते समय मैं उन लोगों से सुझाव लेना पसन्द करती हूँ जिनके विचारों का मैं आदर करती हूँ।
    (ख) कोई ऐसा काम कर बैठने पर जिसे मैं गलत मानती हूँ, मैं यह महसूस करती हूँ कि मैं दोषी हूँ।
48. (क) यदि मुझे कहीं बाहर जाना हो तो मैं उसकी पूरी तैयारी पहले से कर लेना पसन्द करती हूँ।
    (ख) अगर मुझसे कोई गलती हो जाती है तो मैं यह महसूस करती हूँ कि मुझे इसकी सजा भुगतनी चाहिए।
49. (क) मैं ऐसे शब्दों का प्रयोग करना पसन्द करती हूँ जिनका अर्थ लोग अक्सर नहीं जानतें।
    (ख) जिन्हें मैं अपने से बड़ा समझती हूँ उनके सामने भीगी बिल्ली जैसा महसूस करती हूँ।
50. (क) मैं जिम्मेदारियों और बन्धनों से दूर रहना पसन्द करती हूँ।
    (ख) मुझे यह महसूस होता है कि मैं अधिकांश बातों में दूसरों से हीन हूँ।
51. (क) मैं चाहती हूँ कि मैं किसी काम को दूसरों से अधिक अच्छी तरह करने योग्य बन सकूँ।
    (ख) मैं लोगों से दया और सहानुभूति का बर्ताव रखना पसन्द करती हूँ।
52. (क) मैं यह जानना चाहती हूँ कि जिन बातों में मेरी दिलचस्पी है उनके बारे में महान् व्यक्तियों के क्या विचार हैं।
    (ख) आपत्ति के समय मैं अपने मित्रों की सहायता करना पसन्द करती हूँ।
53. (क) मैं जब कुछ लिखती हूँ तो चाहती हूँ कि मेरी लिखावट ठीक-ठाक, साफ और सुव्यवस्थित रहे।
    (ख) मैं उन लोगों की मुसीबतों में काम आना चाहती हूँ जो मुझसे बुरी स्थिति में हैं।
54. (क) मैं ऐसी बातें करना पसन्द करती हूँ जिन्हें लोग सूझ-बूझ की और दिलचस्प समझें।
    (ख) मैं चाहती हूँ कि मेरे मित्र मुझे अपना विश्वासपात्र समझें और अपनी कठिनाइयाँ मुझे बताएँ।
55. (क) मैं चाहती हूँ कि मुझे जो कुछ करना है उसका फैसला बिना किसी दूसरे की मदद के खुद करूँ।
    (ख) अगर मुझे किसी मित्र से दुःख पहुँच जाता है तो मैं उसे भुला देना

पसन्द करती हूँ।

56. (क) मैं जो भी काम हाथ में लेती हूँ उसे सफलतापूर्वक पूरा करना पसन्द करती हूँ।

(ख) मैं यात्रा करना और नई-नई जगहें देखना पसन्द करती हूँ।

57. (क) मैं आदेशों का पालन करना तथा जिस बात की मुझसे उम्मीद की जाती हो उसे पूरा करना पसन्द करती हूँ।

(ख) मैं देश में इधर-उधर जाना और नई-नई जगहों में रहना पसन्द करती हूँ।

58. (क) मैं कोई मुश्किल काम शुरू करने के पहले उसकी एक योजना बना लेना पसन्द करती हूँ।

(ख) मुझे नए-नए लोगों से मिलना-जुलना अच्छा लगता है।

59. (क) दोस्तों की मण्डली में मनोरंजक किस्से और चुटकले सुनना मुझे अच्छा लगता है।

(ख) जो बातें सदा से होती चली आ रही हैं उनकी जगह नई-नई चीजें करना मुझे अच्छा लगता है।

60. (क) मैं चाहती हूँ कि जहाँ जी चाहे, बिना किसी रोक-टोक के आ-जा सकूँ।

(ख) मैं किसी एक ही होटल या जलपान-गृह के बजाए नए-नए होटलों और जलपान-गृहों में जाना पसन्द करती हूँ।

61. (क) मैं चाहती हूँ कि किसी काम को दूसरों से अधिक अच्छी तरह करने के योग्य बना सकूँ।

(ख) जब मुझे कोई काम सौंप दिया जाता है तो मैं उसे तुरन्त शुरू कर देना और जब तक वह पूरा न हो जाए, उसमें लगे रहना पसन्द करती हूँ।

62. (क) अपने से श्रेष्ठ लोग जब किसी काम को अच्छे ढंग से करते हैं तो उनकी तारीफ करने को जी चाहता है।

(ख) मैं एक काम पूरा कर लेने के बाद ही किसी दूसरे काम में हाथ लगाना पसन्द करती हूँ।

63. (क) मैं जब कुछ लिखती हूँ तो चाहती हूँ कि मेरी लिखावट ठीक-ठीक, साफ और सुव्यवस्थित रहे।

(ख) जब मुझे कोई काम सौंप दिया जाता है तो मैं उसे तुरन्त शुरू कर देना और जब तक वह पूरा न हो जाए, उसमें लगे रहना पसन्द करती हूँ।

64. (क) कभी-कभी मैं कोई काम सिर्फ यह देखने के लिए करना पसन्द करती

हूँ कि उसका दूसरों पर क्या असर होता है।

(ख) यह महसूस करते हुए भी कि काम आगे नहीं बढ़ रहा है, मैं उस काम या समस्या में लगे रहना पसन्द करती हूँ

65. (क) मैं चाहती हूँ कि जहाँ जी चाहे, बिना किसी रोक-टोक के आ जा सकूँ।

(ख) किसी काम को पूरा करने के लिए देर तक काम करते रहना मुझे पसन्द है।

66. (क) मैं ऐसे काम करना चाहती हूँ जिन्हें दूसरे लोग समझते हैं कि इनमें बड़ी कुशलता और परिश्रम की आवश्यकता है।

(ख) लड़कों की निगाह में सुन्दर लगना मुझे अच्छा लगता है।

67. (क) अपने समूह का कार्यक्रम दूसरे सदस्यों द्वारा तय किया जाना मुझे पसन्द है।

(ख) मैं लड़कों से दोस्ती करना पसन्द करती हूँ।

68. (क) मैं अपना जीवन-क्रम इस तरह व्यवस्थित कर लेना पसन्द करती हूँ जो बिना किसी खास हेर-फेर के आसानी से चलता रहे।

(ख) मैं ऐसे चुटकले सुनना-सुनाना पसन्द करती हूँ जिनमें प्यार-मुहब्बत की बातें हों।

69. (क) मैं जान-बूझ कर ऐसे प्रश्न पूछना पसन्द करती हूँ जिनका जवाब कोई न दे सके।

(ख) मैं ऐसी कहानियाँ और उपन्यास पढ़ना पसन्द करती हूँ जिनमें काम-वृत्ति (सेक्स) की प्रधानता हो।

70. (क) मुझे ऐसे काम करना पसन्द है जिन्हें रीति-रिवाज के विरुद्ध समझा जाता है।

(ख) मैं ऐसी बहस या बातचीत में भाग लेना पसन्द करती हूँ जिसका विषय काम-वृत्ति (सेक्स) हो।

71. (क) मैं चाहती हूँ कि मुझे यह कहने का अवसर मिले कि मैं किसी मुश्किल काम को बड़ी अच्छी तरह कर सकी हूँ।

(ख) मैं लोगों को जैसा समझती हूँ वैसा उन्हें बता देना पसन्द करती हूँ।

72. (क) मैं जिनकी कद्र करती हूँ उनकी तारीफ करना पसन्द करती हूँ।

(ख) जब मेरा कोई अपमान करता है तो उससे बदला लेने को जी चाहता है।

73. (क) मैं अपनी चिट्ठयों और दूसरे कागज-पत्र कायदे से अलग-अलग

फाइल बनाकर रखना पसन्द करती हूँ।

(ख) मुझे उन विचारों का खण्डन करना अच्छा लगता है जो मेरे अपने विचारों के विरुद्ध हों।

74. (क) मैं ऐसे शब्दों का प्रयोग करना पसन्द करती हूँ जिनका अर्थ लोग अक्सर नहीं जानते।

(ख) मैं कभी-कभी इतना गुस्से में आ जाती हूँ कि चीजों को उठा-पटक और तोड़-फोड़ देने को जी चाहता है।

75. (क) किसी विषय में मैं जो कुछ महसूस करती हूँ उसे कह देना पसन्द करती हूँ।

(ख) जब मेरे साथ कोई गड़बड़ी होती है तो दूसरों को दोष देने को मेरा जी चाहता है।

76. (क) मैं अपने मित्रों के प्रति वफादार रहना पसन्द करती हूँ।

(ख) मैं जिस काम में हाथ लगाती हूँ उसे खूब अच्छी तरह करना पसन्द करती हूँ।

77. (क) मैं अपनी इच्छाओं और अनुभूतियों की छान-बीन करना पसन्द करती हूँ।

(ख) मैं ऐसी पहेलियाँ और समस्याएँ हल करना पसन्द करती हूँ जो दूसरों के लिए मुश्किल पड़ती हैं।

78. (क) अपनी किसी समस्या में उलझे होने पर मैं चाहती हूँ कि मेरे मित्र मेरी कठिनाई समझें और मुझसे सहानुभूति रखें।

(ख) मैं ऐसे कार्य करना चाहती हूँ जिन्हें दूसरे लोग समझते हैं कि इनमें बड़ी कुशलता और परिश्रम की आवश्यकता है।

79. (क) मैं चाहती हूँ कि लोग मुझे अपने झगड़े निपटाने तथ बीच-बचाव करने को कहें।

(ख) मैं चाहती हूँ कि मुझे यह कहने का अवसर मिले कि मैं किसी मुश्किल काम को बड़ी अच्छी तरह कर सकी हूँ।

80. (क) अपनी ही बात रखने की कोशिश करने के बजाए थोड़ा दबकर झगड़ा बचा लेना मुझे ज्यादा अच्छा मालूम होता है।

(ख) मैं चाहती हूँ कि मैं कोई बड़ी किताब लिख सकती।

81. (क) मुझे अपने मित्रों के काम आना अच्छा लगता है।

(ख) मैं जिन लोगों की कद्र करती हूँ उन्हें अपना नेता मानना मुझे पसन्द है।

82. (क) मैं लोगों को परखने में यह देखना चाहती हूँ कि वे कोई काम क्यों करते हैं, न कि वे वास्तव में क्या करते हैं।
 (ख) अमने समूह का कार्यक्रम दूसरे सदस्यों द्वारा तय किया जाना मुझे पसन्द है।
83. (क) किसी काम में असफल होने पर मैं चाहती हूँ कि मेरे मित्र मुझे प्रोत्साहित करें।
 (ख) अपने से श्रेष्ठ लोग जब किसी काम को अच्छे ढंग से करते हैं तो उनकी तारीफ करने को जी चाहता है।
84. (क) मैं लोगों को यह बताना चाहती हूँ कि उन्हें अपना काम किस ढंग से करना चाहिए।
 (ख) मैं जिनकी कद्र करती हूँ उनकी तारीफ करना पसन्द करती हूँ।
85. (क) कोई गलत काम कर देने पर मैं यह महसूस करती हूँ कि मुझे अपनी गलती मान लेनी चाहिए।
 (ख) महान् पुरुषों की जीवनियाँ पढ़ना मुझे अच्छा लगता है।
86. (क) मैं अपने मित्रों के प्रति वफादार रहना पसन्द करती हूँ।
 (ख) मैं जब कुछ लिखती हूँ तो चाहती हूँ कि मेरी लिखावट ठीक-ठीक, साफ और सुव्यवस्थित रहे।
87. (क) मैं पहले से ही यह भाँप लेना चाहती हूँ कि मेरे मित्र किसी परिस्थिति में क्या करने वाले हैं।
 (ख) मुझे किस समय क्या खाना चाहिए यह निश्चित रखना तथा नित्य ठीक समय से खा लेना पसन्द है।
88. (क) मैं चाहती हूँ कि मेरे मित्र मुझसे सहृदयता का बर्ताव करें।
 (ख) किसी काम को शुरू करने के पहले उसकी योजना बना लेना और उसकी तैयारी कर लेना मुझे पसन्द है।
89. (क) अपनी बात का विरोध होने पर मैं उसे ठीक साबित करने की कोशिश करना पसन्द करती हूँ।
 (ख) मुझे किस समय क्या खाना चाहिए यह निश्चित रखना तथा नित्य ठीक समय से खा लेना पसन्द है।
90. (क) कोई गलत काम कर देने पर मैं यह महसूस करती हूँ कि मुझे अपनी गलती मान लेनी चाहिए।
 (ख) यदि मुझे कहीं बाहर जाना हो तो मैं उसकी पूरी तैयारी पहले से कर

लेना पसन्द करती हूँ।

91. (क) मैं अधिक-से-अधिक मित्र बनाना पसन्द करती हूँ।
(ख) मैं अपनी सफलताओं के बारे में बातें करना पसन्द करती हूँ।

92. (क) मैं दूसरों की अनुभूतियों और इच्छाओं की छान-बीन करना पसन्द करती हूँ।
(ख) दूसरों के बीच होने पर मैं ऐसी वेश-भूषा रखना चाहती हूँ कि लोगों की निगाहें मेरी ओर उठें और लोग उस पर अपनी राय दें।

93. (क) जब मैं कभी उदास होती हूँ तो चाहती हूँ कि मेरे मित्र मुझसे सहानुभूति रखें और मेरा उत्साह बढाएँ।
(ख) मैं अपनी सफलताओं के बारे में बातें करना पसन्द करती हूँ।

94. (क) मेरी इच्छा रहती है कि दूसरे लोग मुझे अपना नेता मानें।
(ख) दूसरों के बीच होने पर मैं ऐसी वेश-भूषा रखना चाहती हूँ कि लोगों की निगाहें मेरी ओर उठें और लोग उस पर अपनी राय दें।

95. (क) मुझे यह महसूस होता है कि मैं अधिकांश बातों में दूसरों से हीन हूँ।
(ख) मैं जान-बूझकर ऐसे प्रश्न पूछना पसन्द करती हूँ जिनका जवाब कोई न दे सके।

96. (क) मैं अपनी सभी बातों में मित्रों को शामिल रखना पसन्द करती हूँ।
(ख) मैं अधिकारी-वर्ग के लोगों की आलोचना करना पसन्द करती हूँ।

97. (क) मैं दूसरों के व्यवहारों का अध्ययन और विश्लेषण करना पसन्द करती हूँ।
(ख) बिना इस बात की परवाह किए हुए कि दूसरे क्या सोचेंगे, मैं अपने ढंग से काम करना पसन्द करती हूँ।

98. (क) जब मुझे कोई तकलीफ हो या मैं बीमार पड़ जाऊँ तो मैं यह चाहती हूँ कि मेरे मित्र इसे काफी महत्त्व दें।
(ख) मैं अधिकारी-वर्ग के लोगों की आलोचना करना पसन्द करती हूँ।

99. (क) मैं जो चाहती हूँ वहीं करने के लिए दूसरों को समझा-बुझा कर राजी करना और उन पर अपना प्रभाव डालना पसन्द करती हूँ।
(ख) मैं ऐसे मौकों से बचना चाहती हूँ जहाँ मुझसे रीति-रिवाज निभाने की आशा की जाए।

100. (क) जिन्हें मैं अपने से बड़ा समझती हूँ उनके सामने भीगी-बिल्ली जैसा महसूस करती हूँ।

(ख) मैं जिम्मदारियों और बन्धनों से दूर रहना पसन्द करती हूँ।

101. (क) मैं अपने मित्रों के प्रति उदार रहना पसन्द करती हूँ।
(ख) मैं अपने मित्रों से घनिष्ठ सम्बन्ध रखना पसन्द करती हूँ।

102. (क) मैं अपनी इच्छाओं और अनुभूतियों की छान-बीन करना पसन्द करती हूँ।
(ख) मैं नए दोस्त बनाना पसन्द करती हूँ।

103. (क) किसी परेशानी में पड़ने पर मेरी इच्छा होती है कि मेरे मित्र मेरी सहायता करें।
(ख) मैं कोई काम अकेले करने के बजाए अपने मित्रों के साथ करना पसन्द करती हूँ।

104. (क) मैं चाहती हूँ कि लोग मुझे अपने झगड़े निपटाने तथा बीच-बचाव करने को कहें।
(ख) मैं नए दोस्त बनाना पसन्द करती हूँ।

105. (क) कोई ऐसा काम कर बैठने पर जिसे मैं गलत मानती हूँ, मैं यह महसूस करती हूँ कि मैं दोषी हूँ।
(ख) में कोई काम अकेले करने के बजाए अपने मित्रों के साथ करना पसन्द करती हूँ।

106. (क) मुझे अपने मित्रों को चिट्ठियाँ लिखना अच्छा लगता है।
(ख) मैं पहले से ही यह भाँप लेना चाहती हूँ कि मेरे मित्र किसी परिस्थिति में क्या करने वाले हैं।

107. (क) मैं नए ढंग और नई चलन अपनाना पसन्द करती हूँ।
(ख) मैं दूसरों के व्यवहारों का अध्ययन एवं विश्लेषण करना पसन्द करती हूँ।

108. (क) किसी परेशानी में पड़ने पर मेरी इच्छा होती है कि मेरे मित्र मेरी सहायता करें।
(ख) मैं यह समझना चाहती हूँ कि मेरे मित्र उन समस्याओं के बारे में जिनका वे सामना करते हैं, कैसा अनुभव करते हैं।

109. (क) मैं चाहती हूँ कि अपने संगठन या अपनी मण्डली में मेरा स्थान नेताओं में रहे।
(ख) मैं यह देखना चाहती हूँ कि कोई व्यक्ति किसी खास परिस्थिति में कैसा महसूस करता है।

110. (क) अपनी कोई बात बिगड़ जाने पर मैं यह महसूस करती हूँ कि उसमें मेरा ही दोष सबसे अधिक है।
(ख) मैं लोगों को परखने में यह देखना चाहती हूँ कि वे कोई काम क्यों करते हैं, न कि वे वास्तव में क्या करते हैं।

111. (क) मैं नए दोस्त बनाना पसन्द करती हूँ।
(ख) अपनी किसी समस्या में उलझे होने पर मैं चाहती हूँ कि मेरे मित्र मेरी कठिनाई समझें और मुझसे सहानुभूति रखें।

112. (क) मैं यह देखना चाहती हूँ कि कोई व्यक्ति किसी खास परिस्थिति में कैसा महसूस करता है।
(ख) जब मैं कभी उदास होती हूँ तो चाहती हूँ कि मेरे मित्र मुझसे सहानुभूति रखें और मेरा उत्साह बढ़ाएँ।

113. (क) जब मैं किसी काम में लगी होती हूँ तो चाहती हूँ कि इसमें कोई बाधा या रुकावट न हो।
(ख) मैं चाहती हूँ कि मेरे मित्र मुझसे अधिक-से-अधिक स्नेह रखें।

114. (क) किसी समिति में काम करने पर मैं चाहती हूँ कि मुझे उसका अध्यक्ष बनाया जाए।
(ख) मैं चाहती हूँ कि मेरे मित्र मेरे छोटे-मोटे काम खुशी-खुशी कर दिया करें।

115. (क) मैं ऐसा महसूस करती हूँ कि जो दुःख और मुसीबतें मैंने झेली हैं उनसे मुझे हानि की अपेक्षा लाभ अधिक हुआ है।
(ख) किसी परेशानी में पड़ने पर मेरी इच्छा होती है कि मेरे मित्र मेरी सहायता करें।

116. (क) मैं कोई काम अकेले करने के बजाए अपने मित्रों के साथ करना पसन्द करती हूँ।
(ख) अवसर मिलने पर मैं दूसरों के कामों की देख-रेख करना तथा उन्हें आदेश देना पसन्द करती हूँ।

117. (क) मैं यह समझना चाहती हूँ कि मेरे मित्र उन समस्याओं के बारे में जिनका वे सामना करते हैं, कैसा अनुभव करते हैं।
(ख) किसी मण्डली में काम करने पर मैं चाहती हूँ कि यह निर्णय मैं स्वयं करूँ कि मण्डली का अगला कार्यक्रम क्या हो।

118. (क) जब मुझे कोई तकलीफ हो या मैं बीमार पड़ जाऊँ तो मैं यह चाहती

हूँ कि मेरे मित्र इसे काफी महत्त्व दें।

(ख) मैं चाहती हूँ कि अपने संगठन या अपनी मण्डली में मेरा स्थान नेताओं में रहे।

119. (क) लड़कों की निगाह में सुन्दर लगना मुझे अच्छा लगता है।

(ख) मेरी इच्छा रहती है कि दूसरे लोग मुझे अपना नेता मानें।

120. (क) कोई ऐसा काम कर बैठने पर जिसे मैं गलत मानती हूँ, मैं यह महसूस करती हूँ कि मैं दोषी हूँ।

(ख) अपनी बात का विरोध होने पर मैं उसे ठीक साबित करने की कोशिश करना पसन्द करती हूँ।

121. (क) मुझे अपने मित्रों को चिट्ठियाँ लिखना अच्छा लगता है।

(ख) अपनी ही बात रखने की कोशिश करने के बजाए थोड़ा दबकर झगड़ा बचा लेना मुझे ज्यादा अच्छा मालूम होता है।

122. (क) मैं यह देखना चाहती हूँ कि कोई व्यक्ति किसी खास परिस्थिति में कैसा महसूस करता है।

(ख) मैं ऐसा महसूस करती हूँ कि जो दुःख और मुसीबतें मैंने झेली हैं उनसे मुझे हानि की अपेक्षा लाभ अधिक हुआ है।

123. (क) जब मुझे कोई तकलीफ हो या मैं बीमार पड़ जाऊँ तो मैं यह चाहती हूँ कि मेरे मित्र इसे काफी महत्त्व दें।

(ख) विभिन्न परिस्थितियों को सम्भाल न पाने पर मुझे अपनी अयोग्यता का दुःख होता है।

124. (क) किसी समिति में काम करने पर मैं चाहती हूँ कि मुझे उसका अध्यक्ष बनाया जाए।

(ख) अपनी कोई बात बिगड़ जाने पर मैं यह महसूस करती हूँ कि उसमें मेरा ही दोष सबसे अधिक है।

125. (क) मैं उनकी हँसी उड़ाना पसन्द करती हूँ जिन्हें मैं समझती हूँ कि वे बेवकूफी का काम करते हैं।

(ख) विभिन्न परिस्थितियों को सम्भाल न पाने पर मुझे अपनी अयोग्यता का दुःख होता है।

126. (क) मैं ऐसी मण्डली में रहना पसन्द करती हूँ जहाँ आपस में मैत्री-भाव तथा स्नेह रहे।

(ख) मैं अपने मित्रों से काफी प्रेम-भाव रखना पसन्द करती हूँ।

127. (क) मैं अपने मित्रों के व्यक्तित्व पर विचार करना और यह समझने की कोशिश करना पसन्द करती हूँ कि वे जैसे भी हैं इसका कारण क्या है।
    (ख) अगर मुझे किसी मित्र से दुःख पहुँच जाता है तो मैं उसे भुला देना पसन्द करती हूँ।
128. (क) मैं चाहती हूँ कि मेरे मित्र मुझसे सहृदयता का व्यवहार करें।
    (ख) मैं अपने मित्रों के प्रति उदार रहना पसन्द करती हूँ।
129. (क) अवसर मिलने पर मैं दूसरों के कामों की देख-रेख करना तथा उन्हें आदेश देना पसन्द करती हूँ।
    (ख) मैं अपने मित्रों के काम कर देना पसन्द करती हूँ।
130. (क) कोई गलत काम कर देने पर मैं यह महसूस करती हूँ कि मुझे अपनी गलती मान लेनी चाहिए।
    (ख) मैं लोगों से दया और सहानुभूति का बर्ताव रखना पसन्द करती हूँ।
131. (क) मैं अपने मित्रों से घनिष्ठ सम्बन्ध रखना पसन्द करती हूँ।
    (ख) मैं ऐसी चीजें करना पसन्द करती हूँ जिनमें कोई नई बात हो।
132. (क) मैं पहले से ही यह भाँप लेना चाहती हूँ कि मेरे मित्र किसी परिस्थिति में क्या करने वाले हैं।
    (ख) मैं नए-नए कामों में हाथ लगाना और उन्हें आजमाना पसन्द करती हूँ।
133. (क) जब मैं कभी उदास होती हूँ तो चाहती हूँ कि मेरे मित्र मुझसे सहानुभूति रखें और मेरा उत्साह बढाएँ।
    (ख) मैं नए ढंग और नई चलन अपनाना पसन्द करती हूँ।
134. (क) मैं लोगों को यह बताना चाहती हूँ कि उन्हें अपना काम किस ढंग से करना चाहिए।
    (ख) मैं ऐसी चीजें करना पसन्द करती हूँ जिनमें कोई नई बात हो।
135. (क) अपनी कोई बात बिगड़ जाने पर मैं यह महसूस करती हूँ कि उसमें मेरा ही दोष सबसे अधिक है।
    (ख) मैं किसी एक ही होटल या जलपान-गृह के बजाए नए-नए होटलों और जलपान-गृहों में जाना पसन्द करती हूँ।
136. (क) मुझे अपने मित्रों कें काम आना अच्छा लगता है।
    (ख) मैं जिस काम को शुरू करती हूँ उसे पूरा कर देना ही पसन्द करती हूँ।
137. (क) मैं अपने मित्रों के व्यक्तित्व पर विचार करना और यह समझने की कोशिश करना पसन्द करती हूँ कि वे जैसे भी हैं इसका कारण क्या है।

(ख) जब मैं किसी काम में लगी होती हूँ तो चाहती हूँ कि इसमें कोई बाधा या रुकावट न हो।

138. (क) अपनी किसी समस्या में उलझे होने पर मैं चाहती हूँ कि मेरे मित्र मेरी कठिनाई समझें और मुझसे सहानुभूति रखें।

(ख) मैं चाहती हूँ कि बिना ध्यान बँटाए घंटों काम करती रहूँ।

139. (क) किसी मण्डली में काम करने पर मैं चाहती हूँ कि यह निर्णय मैं स्वयं करूँ कि मण्डली का अगला कार्यक्रम क्या हो।

(ख) यह महसूस करते हुए भी कि काम आगे नहीं बढ़ रहा है, मैं उस काम या समस्या में लगे रहना पसन्द करती हूँ।

140. (क) अगर मुझसे कोई गलती हो जाती है तो मैं यह महसूस करती हूँ कि मुझे इसकी सजा भुगतनी चाहिए।

(ख) मैं किसी समस्या या पहेली में उस समय तक लगे रहना पसन्द करती हूँ जब तक कि वह हल न हो जाए।

141. (क) मैं अधिक-से-अधिक मित्र बनाना पसन्द करती हूँ।

(ख) मैं ऐसे उत्सवों तथा कार्यक्रमों में भाग लेना पसन्द करती हूँ जिनमें लड़के भी शामिल हों।

142. (क) मैं यह समझना चाहती हूँ कि मेरे मित्र उन समस्याओं के बारे में जिनका वे सामना करते हैं, कैसा अनुभव करते हैं।

(ख) मुझे सुन्दर लड़कों से मिलना-जुलना अच्छा लगता है।

143. (क) जब मैं बीमार होती हूँ तो चाहती हूँ कि मेरे मित्र मेरे लिए दुःखी हों।

(ख) मैं लड़कों से दोस्ती करना पसन्द करती हूँ।

144. (क) मैं चाहती हूँ कि अपने संगठन या अपनी मण्डली में मेरा स्थान नेताओं में रहे।

(ख) लड़कों के साथ कहीं जाना मुझे अच्छा लगता है।

145. (क) विभिन्न परिस्थितियों को सम्भाल न पाने पर मुझे अपनी अयोग्यता का दुःख होता है।

(ख) लड़कों के साथ गप-शप करना मुझे अच्छा लगता है।

146. (क) मैं अपनी सभी बातों में मित्रों को शामिल रखना पसन्द करती हूँ।

(ख) मैं उस आदमी की खुलेआम आलोचना करना पसन्द करती हूँ जिसे मैं इसके योग्य समझती हूँ।

147. (क) मैं दूसरों की अनुभूतियों और इच्छाओं की छान-बीन करना पसन्द करती हूँ।

(ख) जब मैं दूसरों से असहमत होती हूँ तो उन्हें यह बात दो-टूक बता देना पसन्द करती हूँ।

148. (क) जब मैं बीमार होती हूँ तो चाहती हूँ कि मेरे मित्र मेरे लिए दुखी हों।
(ख) मैं हत्या तथा मार-काट की खबरें पढ़ना और सुनना पसन्द करती हूँ।

149. (क) मेरी इच्छा रहती है कि दूसरे लोग मुझे अपना नेता मानें।
(ख) मैं उनकी हँसी उड़ाना पसन्द करती हूँ जिन्हें मैं समझती हूँ कि वे बेवकूफी का काम करते हैं।

150. (क) जिन्हें मैं अपने से बड़ा समझती हूँ उनके सामने भीगी बिल्ली जैसा महसूस करती हूँ।
(ख) मैं कभी-कभी इतना गुस्से में आ जाती हूँ कि चीजों को उठा-पटक और तोड़-फोड़ देने को जी चाहता है।

151. (क) मैं मित्रों के दुख-दर्द में शरीक होना पसन्द करती हूँ।
(ख) मैं जो भी काम हाथ में लेती हूँ उसे सफलतापूर्वक पूरा करना पसन्द करती हूँ।

152. (क) मैं यात्रा करना और नई-नई जगहें देखना पसन्द करती हूँ।
(ख) मैं चाहती हूँ कि मैं कोई ऐसा काम करूँ जिसका बड़ा महत्त्व हो।

153. (क) मैं जिस काम को शुरू करती हूँ उसे पूरा कर देना ही पसन्द करती हूँ।
(ख) मैं चाहती हूँ कि मैं किसी काम को दूसरों से अधिक अच्छी तरह करने के योग्य बन सकूँ।

154. (क) मैं ऐसे चुटकले सुनना-सुनाना पसन्द करती हूँ जिनमें प्यार-मुहब्बत की बातें हों।
(ख) मैं चाहती हूँ कि मुझे यह कहने का अवसर मिले कि मैं किसी मुश्किल काम को बड़ी अच्छी तरह कर सकी हूँ।

155. (क) जब मैं दूसरों से असहमत होती हूँ तो उन्हें यह बात दो-टूक बता देना पसन्द करती हूँ।
(ख) मैं ऐसे काम करना चाहती हूँ जिन्हें लोग समझते हैं कि इनमें बड़ी कुशलता और परिश्रम की आवश्यकता है।

156. (क) मैं अपने मित्रों से काफी प्रेम-भाव रखना पसन्द करती हूँ।
(ख) मैं जिन लोगों की कद्र करती हूँ उन्हें अपना नेता मानना मुझे पसन्द है।

157. (क) मुझे नए-नए लोगों से मिलना-जुलना अच्छा लगता है।
(ख) मैं रीति-रिवाज के अनुकूल रहना पसन्द करती हूँ और ऐसा कुछ नहीं

करना चाहती जिसे आदरणीय जन परम्परा-विरुद्ध समझते हैं।

158. (क) मैं जो भी काम हाथ में लेती हूँ उसे पूरे परिश्रम से करना पसन्द करती हूँ।

(ख) महान् पुरुषों की जीवनियाँ पढ़ना मुझे अच्छा लगता है।

159. (क) मुझे सुन्दर लड़कों से मिलना-जुलना अच्छा लगता है।

(ख) अपने समूह का कार्यक्रम दूसरे सदस्यों द्वारा तय किया जाना मुझे पसन्द है।

160. (क) मुझे उन विचारों का खण्डन करना अच्छा लगता है जो मेरे अपने विचारों के विरुद्ध हों।

(ख) मैं जिनकी कद्र करती हूँ उनकी तारीफ करना पसन्द करती हूँ।

161. (क) आपत्ति के समय मैं अपने मित्रों की सहायता करना पसन्द करती हूँ।

(ख) कोई काम शुरू करने से पहले मैं उसके हर पहलू को सोच-समझ लेना पसन्द करती हूँ।

162. (क) मैं नए-नए कामों में हाथ लगाना और उन्हें आजमाना पसन्द करती हूँ।

(ख) मैं अपनी काम करने की जगह या मेज पर सब चीजें ढंग से सजाकर रखना पसन्द करती हूँ।

163. (क) मैं किसी समस्या या पहेली में उस समय तक लगे रहना पसन्द करती हूँ जब तक कि वह हल न हो जाए।

(ख) मैं अपनी चिट्ठियाँ और दूसरे कागज-पत्र कायदे से अलग-अलग फाइल बनाकर रखना पसन्द करती हूँ।

164. (क) मैं ऐसे उत्सवों तथा कार्यक्रमों में भाग लेना पसन्द करती हूँ जिनमें लड़के भी शामिल हों।

(ख) किसी काम को शुरू करने के पहले उसकी योजना बना लेना और उसकी तैयारी कर लेना मुझे पसन्द है।

165. (क) मैं लोगों को जैसा समझती हूँ वैसा उन्हें बता देना पसन्द करती हूँ।

(ख) मुझे किस समय क्या खाना खाना चाहिए यह निश्चित रखना तथा नित्य ठीक समय से खा लेना पसन्द है।

166. (क) मैं अपने मित्रों के काम कर देना पसन्द करती हूँ।

(ख) मैं ऐसी बातें करना पसन्द करती हूँ जिन्हें लोग सूझ-बूझ की और दिलचस्प समझें।

167. (क) मैं अपने दैनिक कार्यक्रम में हेर-फेर करते रहना पसन्द करती हूँ।

(ख) कभी-कभी मैं कोई काम सिर्फ यह देखने के लिए करती हूँ कि उसका दूसरों पर क्या असर होता है।

168. (क) यह महसूस करते हुए भी कि काम आगे नहीं बढ़ रहा है, मैं उस काम या समस्या में लगे रहना पसन्द करती हूँ।

(ख) समूह में मैं यह चाहती हूँ कि सब लोग मेरी ही ओर ध्यान दें।

169. (क) मैं ऐसी बहस या बातचीत में भाग लेना पसन्द करती हूँ जिसका विषय काम-वृत्ति (सेक्स) हो।

(ख) मैं ऐसे शब्दों का प्रयोग करना पसन्द करती हूँ जिनका अर्थ लोग अक्सर नहीं जानते।

170. (क) जब मेरे साथ कोई गड़बड़ी हो जाती है तो दूसरों को दोष को मेरा जी चाहता है।

(ख) दूसरों के सामने मैं अपनी बहादुरी और अपने जीवन की आश्चर्यजनक बातों की दास्तान सुनाना पसन्द करती हूँ।

171. (क) मैं चाहती हूँ कि मेरे मित्र मुझे अपना विश्वासपात्र समझें और अपनी कठिनाइयाँ मुझे बताएँ।

(ख) मुझे जो कुछ करना है उसके करने में मैं आजादी महसूस करना चाहती हूँ।

172. (क) मैं अपने दैनिक कार्यक्रम में हेर-फेर करते रहना पसन्द करती हूँ।

(ख) मैं ऐसे मौकों से बचना चाहती हूँ जहाँ मुझसे रीति-रिवाज निभाने की आशा की जाए।

173. (क) किसी काम को पूरा करने के लिए देर तक काम करते रहना मुझे पसन्द है।

(ख) मैं चाहती हूँ कि जहाँ जी चाहे, बिना किसी रोक-टोक के आ जा सकूँ।

174. (क) मैं ऐसी कहानियाँ और उपन्यास पढ़ना पसन्द करती हूँ जिनमें काम-वृत्ति (सेक्स) की प्रधानता हो।

(ख) किसी विषय में मैं जो महसूस करती हूँ उसे कह देना पसन्द करती हूँ।

175. (क) मैं कभी-कभी इतना गुस्से में आ जाती हूँ कि चीजों को उठा-पटक और तोड़-फोड़ देने को जी चाहता है।

(ख) मुझे ऐसे काम करना पसन्द है जिन्हें रीति-रिवाज के विरुद्ध समझा जाता है।

176. (क) मैं अपने मित्रों के प्रति उदार रहना पसन्द करती हूँ।

(ख) मैं अपने मित्रों से घनिष्ठ सम्बन्ध रखना पसन्द करती हूँ।

177. (क) मैं देश में इधर-उधर जाना और नई-नई जगहों में रहना पसन्द करती हूँ।

(ख) मैं ऐसी मण्डली में रहना पसन्द करती हूँ जहाँ आपस में मैत्रीभाव तथा स्नेह रहे।

178. (क) मैं जो भी काम अपने हाथ में लेती हूँ उसे पूरे परिश्रम से करना पसन्द करती हूँ।

(ख) मैं अपने मित्रों के प्रति वफादार रहना पसन्द करती हूँ।

179. (क) लड़कों के साथ कहीं जाना मुझे अच्छा लगता है।

(ख) मैं अपनी सभी बातों में मित्रों को शामिल रखना पसन्द करती हूँ।

180. (क) जब मेरा कोई अपमान करता है तो उससे बदला लेने को जी चाहता है।

(ख) मैं अधिक-से-अधिक मित्र बनाना पसन्द करती हूँ।

181. (क) मैं अपने मित्रों के काम कर देना पसन्द करती हूँ।

(ख) मैं अपने को दूसरे की परिस्थिति में रखकर यह समझना चाहती हूँ कि उस स्थिति में मुझे कैसा लगता है।

182. (क) मैं नए ढंग और नए चलन अपनाना पसन्द करती हूँ।

(ख) मैं दूसरों के व्यवहार का अध्ययन और विश्लेषण करना पसन्द करती हूँ।

183. (क) मैं चाहती हूँ कि बिना ध्यान बँटाए घंटों काम करती रहूँ।

(ख) मैं अपनी अनुभूतियों और इच्छाओं की छानबीन करना पसन्द करती हूँ।

184. (क) लड़कों की निगाह में सुन्दर लगना मुझे अच्छा लगता है।

(ख) मैं दूसरों की इच्छाओं और अनुभूतियों की छानबीन करना पसन्द करती हूँ।

185. (क) मैं उस आदमी की खुलेआम आलोचना करना पसन्द करती हूँ जिसे मैं इसके योग्य समझती हूँ।

(ख) मैं लोगों को परखने में यह देखना चाहती हूँ कि वे कोई काम क्यों करते हैं, न कि वास्तव में क्या करते हैं।

186. (क) मैं चाहती हूँ कि मेरे मित्र मुझे अपना विश्वासपात्र समझें और अपनी कठिनाइयाँ मुझे बताएँ।

(ख) मैं चाहती हूँ कि मेरे मित्र मुझसे अधिक-से-अधिक स्नेह रखें।

187. (क) जो बातें सदा से होती चली आ रही हैं उनकी जगह नई-नई चीजें करना मुझे अच्छा लगता है।

(ख) किसी काम में असफल होने पर मैं चाहती हूँ कि मेरे मित्र मुझे प्रोत्साहित करें।

188. (क) जब मैं किसी काम में लगी होती हूँ तो चाहती हूँ कि इसमें कोई बाधा या रुकावट न हो।

(ख) मैं चाहती हूँ कि मेरे मित्र मुझसे अधिक-से-अधिक स्नेह रखें।

189. (क) लड़कों के साथ गप-शप करना मुझे अच्छा लगता है।

(ख) जब मैं बीमार होती हूँ तो चाहती हूँ कि मेरे मित्र मेरे लिए दुखी हों।

190. (क) जब मैं दूसरों से असहमत होती हूँ तो उन्हें यह बात दो-टूक बता देना पसन्द करती हूँ।

(ख) मैं चाहती हूँ कि मेरे मित्र मेरे छोटे-मोटे काम खुशी-खुशी कर दिया करें।

191. (क) अगर मुझे किसी मित्र से दुःख पहुँच जाता है तो मैं उसे भुला देना पसन्द करती हूँ।

(ख) मैं चाहती हूँ कि लोग मुझे अपने झगड़े निपटाने तथ बीच-बचाव करने को कहें।

192. (क) मैं अपने दैनिक कार्यक्रम में हेर-फेर करते रहना पसन्द करती हूँ।

(ख) किसी मण्डली में काम करने पर मैं चाहती हूँ कि यह निर्णय मैं स्वयं करूँ कि मण्डली का अगला कार्यक्रम क्या हो।

193. (क) जब मैं किसी काम में लगी होती हूँ तो चाहती हूँ कि इसमें कोई बाधा या रुकावट न हो।

(ख) अपनी बात का विरोध होने पर मैं उसे ठीक साबित करने की कोशिश करना पसन्द करती हूँ।

194. (क) लड़कों की निगाह में सुन्दर लगना मुझे अच्छा लगता है।

(ख) मेरी इच्छा रहती है कि दूसरे लोग मुझे अपना नेता मानें।

195. (क) मैं हत्या तथा मार-काट की खबरें पढ़ना और सुनना पसन्द करती हूँ।

(ख) मैं जो चाहती हूँ वही करने के लिए दूसरों को समझा-बुझाकर राजी करना और उन पर अपना प्रभाव डालना पसन्द करती हूँ।

196. (क) मैं अपने मित्रों के प्रति उदार रहना पसन्द करती हूँ।

(ख) अपनी ही बात रखने की कोशिश करने के बजाए थोड़ा दबकर झगड़ा बचा लेना मुझे ज्यादा अच्छा मालूम होता है।

197. (क) मैं नए ढंग और नई चलन अपनाना पसन्द करती हूँ।

(ख) मैं ऐसा महसूस करती हूँ कि जो दुःख और मुसीबतें मैंने झेली हैं उनसे मुझे हानि की अपेक्षा लाभ अधिक हुआ है।

198. (क) जब मुझे कोई काम सौंप दिया जाता है तो मैं उसे तुरन्त शुरू कर देना और जब तक वह पूरा न हो जाए, उसमें लगे रहना पसन्द करती हूँ।

(ख) कोई गलत काम कर देने पर मैं यह महसूस करती हूँ कि मुझे अपनी गलती मान लेनी चाहिए।

199. (क) मैं ऐसी कहानियाँ और उपन्यास पढ़ना पसन्द करती हूँ जिनमें कामवृत्ति (सेक्स) की प्रधानता हो।

(ख) मुझे यह महसूस होता है कि मैं अधिकांश बातों में दूसरों से हीन हूँ।

200. (क) मैं उनकी हँसी उड़ाना पसन्द करती हूँ जिन्हें मैं समझती हूँ कि वे बेवकूफी का काम करते हैं।

(ख) विभिन्न परिस्थितियों को सम्भाल न पाने पर मुझे अपनी अयोग्यता का दुःख होता है।

201. (क) मैं चाहती हूँ कि मैं किसी काम को दूसरों से अधिक अच्छी तरह करने के योग्य बन सकूँ।

(ख) मैं लोगों से दया और सहानुभूति का बर्ताव रखना पसन्द करती हूँ।

202. (क) मैं यात्रा करना और नई-नई जगहें देखना पसन्द करती हूँ।

(ख) मैं उन लोगों की मुसीबतों में काम आना चाहती हूँ जो मुझसे बुरी स्थिति में हैं।

203. (क) मैं जो भी काम हाथ में लेती हूँ उसे पूरे परिश्रम से करना पसन्द करती हूँ।

(ख) आपत्ति के समय मैं अपने मित्रों की सहायता करना पसन्द करती हूँ।

204. (क) मैं ऐसे उत्सवों तथा कार्यक्रमों में भाग लेना पसन्द करती हूँ जिनमें लड़के भी शामिल हों।

(ख) मैं अपने मित्रों से काफी प्रेम-भाव रखना पसन्द करती हूँ।

205. (क) मुझे उन विचारों का खण्डन करना अच्छा लगता है जो मेरे अपने विचारों के विरुद्ध हों।

(ख) मैं उन लोगों की मुसीबतों में काम आना चाहती हूँ जो मुझसे बुरी

स्थिति में हैं।

206. (क) मैं लोगों से दया और सहानुभूति का बर्ताव रखना पसन्द करती हूँ।
(ख) मैं देश में इधर-उधर जाना और नई-नई जगहों पर रहना पसन्द करती हूँ।

207. (क) मैं आदेशों का पालन करना तथा जिस बात की मुझसे उम्मीद की जाती हो उसे पूरा करना पसन्द करती हूँ।
(ख) मैं देश में इधर-उधर जाना और नई-नई जगहों पर रहना पसन्द करती हूँ।

208. (क) मैं एक काम को पूरा कर लेने के बाद ही किसी दूसरे काम में हाथ लगाना पसन्द करती हूँ।
(ख) जो बातें सदा से होती चली आ रही हैं उनकी जगह नई-नई चीजें करना मुझे अच्छा लगता है।

209. (क) मुझे सुन्दर लड़कों से मिलना-जुलना अच्छा लगता है।
(ख) मैं किसी एक ही होटल या जलपान-गृह के बजाए नए-नए होटलों और जलपान-गृहों में जाना पसन्द करती हूँ।

210. (क) मैं हत्या तथा मार-काट की खबरें पढ़ना और सुनना पसन्द करती हूँ।
(ख) मैं अपने दैनिक कार्यक्रम में हेर-फेर करते रहना पसन्द करती हूँ।

211. (क) मैं मित्रों के दुख-दर्द में शरीक होना पसन्द करती हूँ।
(ख) मैं जिस काम को शुरू करती हूँ उसे पूरा कर देना ही पसन्द करती हूँ।

212. (क) मुझे नए-नए लोगों से मिलना-जुलना अच्छा लगता है।
(ख) मैं एक काम कर लेने के बाद ही किसी दूसरे काम में हाथ लगाना पसन्द करती हूँ।

213. (क) मैं जब कुछ लिखती हूँ तो चाहती हूँ कि मेरी लिखावट ठीक-ठीक, साफ और सुव्यवस्थित हो।
(ख) जब मुझे कोई काम सौंप दिया जाता है तो मैं उसे तुरन्त शुरू कर देना और जब तक वह पूरा न हो जाए, उसमें लगे रहना पसन्द करती हूँ।

214. (क) मैं ऐसे चुटकले सुनना-सुनाना पसन्द करती हूँ जिनमें प्यार-मुहब्बत की बातें हों।
(ख) मैं चाहती हूँ कि बिना ध्यान बँटाए घंटों काम करती रहूँ।

215. (क) जब कोई मेरा अपमान करता है तो उससे बदला लेने को जी चाहता है।

(ख) मैं किसी समस्या या पहेली में उस समय तक लगे रहना पसन्द करती हूँ जब तक कि हल न हो जाए।

216. (क) अगर मुझे किसी मित्र से दुःख पहुँच जाता है तो मैं उसे भुला देना पसन्द करती हूँ।

(ख) मैं लड़कों से दोस्ती करना पसन्द करती हूँ।

217. (क) मैं ऐसी चीजें करना पसन्द करती हूँ जिनमें कोई नई बात हो।

(ख) मैं ऐसे उत्सवों तथा कार्यक्रमों में भाग लेना पसन्द करती हूँ जिनमें लड़के भी शामिल हों।

218. (क) किसी काम को पूरा करने के लिए देर तक काम करते रहना मुझे पसन्द है।

(ख) लड़कों के साथ कहीं जाना मुझे अच्छा लगता है।

219. (क) मैं जान-बूझ कर ऐसे प्रश्न पूछना पसन्द करती हूँ जिनका जवाब कोई न दे सके।

(ख) मैं ऐसी कहानियाँ और उपन्यास पढ़ना पसन्द करती हूँ जिनमें कामवृत्ति (सेक्स) की प्रधानता हो।

220. (क) जब मेरे साथ कोई गड़बड़ी होती है तो दूसरों को दोष देने को मेरा जी चाहता है।

(ख) मैं ऐसी बहस या बातचीत में भाग लेना पसन्द करती हूँ जिसका विषय काम-वृत्ति (सेक्स) हो।

221. (क) मैं मित्रों के दुख-दर्द में शरीक होना पसन्द करती हूँ।

(ख) मुझे उन विचारों का खण्डन करना अच्छा लगता है जो मरे अपने विचारों के विरुद्ध हों।

222. (क) मैं नए-नए कामों में हाथ लगाना और उन्हें आजमाना पसन्द करती हूँ।

(ख) मैं लोगों को जैसा समझती हूँ वैसा उन्हें बता देना पसन्द करती हूँ।

223. (क) किसी काम को पूरा करने के लिए देर तक काम करते रहना मुझे पसन्द है।

(ख) मैं उस आदमी की खुलेआम आलोचना करना पसन्द करती हूँ जिसे मैं इसके योग्य समझती हूँ।

224. (क) लड़कों के साथ गप-शप करना मुझे अच्छा लगता है।

(ख) मैं उनकी हँसी उड़ाना पसन्द करती हूँ जिन्हें मैं समझती हूँ कि वे बेवकूफी का काम करते हैं।

225. (क) किसी विषय में मैं जो कुछ महसूस करती हूँ उसे कह देना पसन्द करती हूँ।
(ख) जब मेरे साथ कोई गड़बड़ी हो जाती है तो दूसरों को दोष देने को मेरा जी चाहता है।

आपकी पसन्द : एक अनुसूची (उत्तर-पत्र)

नाम .... स्त्री/पुरुष कक्षा......... विभाग/कॉलेज....................
आयु.................... वर्ष/मास विश्वविद्यालय..
ता. .... 2000........ स्थान..............................

अनुसूची में दिये प्रत्येक क्रमांक के अनुसार 'उत्तर-पत्र' में भी वही क्रमांक ढूंढिये। उसके आगे दिये 'क' या 'ख' को, जिसे आपने चुना है गोल निशान से घेरिये।

1. क ख	17. क ख	33. क ख
2. क ख	18. क ख	34. क ख
3. क ख	19. क ख	35. क ख
4. क ख	20. क ख	36. क ख
5. क ख	21. क ख	37. क ख
6. क ख	22. क ख	38. क ख
7. क ख	23. क ख	39. क ख
8. क ख	24. क ख	40. क ख
9. क ख	25. क ख	41. क ख
10. क ख	26. क ख	42. क ख
11. क ख	27. क ख	43. क ख
12. क ख	28. क ख	44. क ख
13. क ख	29. क ख	45. क ख
14. क ख	30. क ख	46. क ख
15. क ख	31. क ख	47. क ख
16. क ख	32. क ख	48. क ख

49. क ख
50. क ख
51. क ख
52. क ख
53. क ख
54. क ख
55. क ख
56. क ख
57. क ख
58. क ख
59. क ख
60. क ख
61. क ख
62. क ख
63. क ख
64. क ख
65. क ख
66. क ख
67. क ख
68. क ख
69. क ख
70. क ख
71. क ख
72. क ख
73. क ख
74. क ख
75. क ख
76. क ख
77. क ख
78. क ख
79. क ख
80. क ख
81. क ख
82. क ख
83. क ख
84. क ख
85. क ख
86. क ख
87. क ख
88. क ख
89. क ख
90. क ख
91. क ख
92. क ख
93. क ख
94. क ख
95. क ख
96. क ख
97. क ख
98. क ख
99. क ख
100. क ख
101. क ख
102. क ख
103. क ख
104. क ख
105. क ख
106. क ख
107. क ख
108. क ख
109. क ख
110. क ख
111. क ख
112. क ख
113. क ख
114. क ख
115. क ख
116. क ख
117. क ख
118. क ख
119. क ख
120. क ख
121. क ख
122. क ख
123. क ख
124. क ख
125. क ख
126. क ख
127. क ख
128. क ख
129. क ख
130. क ख
131. क ख
132. क ख
133. क ख
134. क ख
135. क ख
136. क ख
137. क ख
138. क ख
139. क ख
140. क ख
141. क ख

142.	क	ख	170.	क	ख	198.	क	ख
143.	क	ख	171.	क	ख	199.	क	ख
144.	क	ख	172.	क	ख	200.	क	ख
145.	क	ख	173.	क	ख	201.	क	ख
146.	क	ख	174.	क	ख	202.	क	ख
147.	क	ख	175.	क	ख	203.	क	ख
148.	क	ख	176.	क	ख	204.	क	ख
149.	क	ख	177.	क	ख	205.	क	ख
150.	क	ख	178.	क	ख	206.	क	ख
151.	क	ख	179.	क	ख	207.	क	ख
152.	क	ख	180.	क	ख	208.	क	ख
153.	क	ख	181.	क	ख	209.	क	ख
154.	क	ख	182.	क	ख	210.	क	ख
155.	क	ख	183.	क	ख	211.	क	ख
156.	क	ख	184.	क	ख	212.	क	ख
157.	क	ख	185.	क	ख	213.	क	ख
158.	क	ख	186.	क	ख	214.	क	ख
159.	क	ख	187.	क	ख	215.	क	ख
160.	क	ख	188.	क	ख	216.	क	ख
161.	क	ख	189.	क	ख	217.	क	ख
162.	क	ख	190.	क	ख	218.	क	ख
163.	क	ख	191.	क	ख	219.	क	ख
164.	क	ख	192.	क	ख	220.	क	ख
165.	क	ख	193.	क	ख	221.	क	ख
166.	क	ख	194.	क	ख	222.	क	ख
167.	क	ख	195.	क	ख	223.	क	ख
168.	क	ख	196.	क	ख	224.	क	ख
169.	क	ख	197.	क	ख	225.	क	ख

इसके नीचे कुछ न लिखिये

□	□	□	□	□	□	□	□	□	□	□	□	□	□	□
1	2	3	4	5	6	7	8	9	10	11	12	13	14	15

इन खानों में कुछ न लिखिये

n	*r*	*c*	*s*
ach	....	....	....
def	....	....	....
ord	....	....	....
exh	....	....	....
aut	....	....	....
aff	....	....	....
int	....	....	....
suc	....	....	....
dom	....	....	....
aba	....	....	....
nur	....	....	....
chg	....	....	....
end	....	....	....
het	....	....	....
agg	....	....	....
con	....	....	....

Bibliography

Agrawal, T.D. & Upadhyaya, S.N. (1983). Sex and age differences in affiliation behaviour. *Psychological Studies,* 28, 1.

Alper, T.G. & Greenberger, E. (1967). Relationship of picture structure to achievement motivation in college women. *Journal of Personality and Social Pyschology,* 7, 362-371.

Atkinson, J.W. (ed.) (1958). *Motives in Fantasy : Action and Society.* Princeton, J.J. : Van Nostrand.

Bachtold, L.M. & Werner, E.E. (1972). Personality characteristics of women scientists. *Psychological Reports,* 31, 391-396.

Bardwick, J. (1971). *Psychology of Women.* New York : Harper & Row.

Bart, P. (1970). Mother Portnoy's complaints. *Trans-action,* 9, 69-74.

Baruch, R. (1967). The achievement motive in women : Implications for career development. *Journal of Personality and Social Psychology,* 5, 260-267.

Baumrind, D. (1971). Current patterns of parental authority. *Developmental Psychology Monograph,* 1(1), 4.

Baumrind, D. & Black, A.E. (1967). Socialization practices associated with dimensions of competence in preschool boys and girls. *Child Development,* 38, 291-327.

Bem, S.L. (1974). The measurement of psychological androgyny. *Journal of Consulting and Clinical Psychology,* 42, 155-162.

Bem, S.L. (1975). Sex-role adaptability : One consequence of psychological androgyny. *Journal of Personality and Social Psychology,* 31, 634–643.

Bernard, J. (1972). *The Future of Marriage.* New York : Bantam Books.

Biller, H.B. (1971). An AFDC mothers groups : An exploratory effort in community mental health. *Family Coordinator,* 21, 287–290.

Birnbaum, J.L. (1971). Life patterns, personality style and self-esteem in gifted family oriented and career committed women. Unpublished Doctoral Dissertation, University of Michigan.

Blake, J. (1969). Population policy for Americans : Is the government being misled? *Science,* 164, 522-529.

Bledsol, J.C. (1978). Vocational orientation of college women as related to selected personality characteristics. *Psychological Reports,* 42, 835-841.

Borgatta, E. & Evans, R. (1967). Behavioural and personality expectations associated with status positions. *Multivariate Behavioural Research.* 2, 153–174.

Brandt, S.J. (1978). Psychological correlates of occupational choice in women : *Dissertation Abstracts International,* 38(7).

Brown, N.E. (1985). Psychological variables that discriminate between midlife homemakers and homemaker graduate students as an aid to lifespan counselling. Dissertation Abstracts International, Sec. A. *Humanities and Social Science,* 45(9).

Broverman, I.K.; Vogel, S.R.; Broverman, D.M.; Clarkson, F.E. & Rosenkrantz, P.S. (1972). Sex-role stereotypes: A current appraisal. *Journal of Social Issues,* 28, 59-78.

Burns, P.J.H. (1976). Profiles of achievement related behaviours in career and non-career women. *Dissertation Abstracts International,* Sec. B., 37(5).

Cooley, C.H. (1902). *Human Nature and the Social* Order. N.Y. : Scribner.

Coopersmith, S. (1967). *The Antecedents of Self-esteem.* San Francisco: W.H. Freeman.

Crandall, V.C. & Battle, E.S. (1970). The antecedents and adults correlates of academic and intellectual achievement effort. In J.P. Hill (Ed.), *Minnesota Symposia on Child Psychology,* Vol. 4, Minnesota Press, 36-95.

Crandall, V.J. (1963). Achievement. In H.W. Stevenson (Ed.) *Child Psychology : The 62nd Yearbook of the National Society for the Study of Education,* Part I. Chicago : University of Chicago Press, 416-459.

Crandall, V.J. & Rabson, A. (1960). Children's repetition choices in an intellectual achievement situation following success and failure. *Journal of Genetic Psychology,* 97, 161-168.

Crowther, B. & More, D. (1972). Occupational stereotyping on initial impressions. *Journal of Vocational Behaviour.* 2, 84-87.

De Man, A.F. & Benoit, R. (1982). Self-esteem in feminist and non-feminist French-Canadian Man. *Journal of Psychology,* 111(1), 3.7.

Desai, N. & Krishnaraj, M. (1987). *Women and Society in India.* Ajanta Publications, New Delhi.

Donelson, E. & Gullahorn, J. (1977). *Women : A Psychological Perspective.* New York : Wiley.

Dube, S.C. (1963). Men's and women's roles in India. *Women in the New Asia* (Eds.) Barbara E. Ward, Paris, UNESCO.

Erdwins, C.J. & Mellinger, J.C. (1984). Mid-Life women: Relation of age and role to personality. *Journal of Personality and Social Psychology,* 47(2), 390–395.

Feld, S. (1963). Feelings of adjustment. In F.I. Nye & L.W. Hoffman (Eds.), *The Employed Mother in America.* Chicago: Rand McNally.

Ferguson, G.A. (1971). *Statistical Analysis in Psychology and Education.* Third Edition, McGraw-Hill, Inc.

Festinger, L. & Katz. D. (Eds.) (1953). *Research Methods in Behavioural Sciences.* New York : The Dryden Press.

Fidell, L.S. (1976). Employment status, role dissatisfaction and the housewife syndrome. *Psychology of Women Quarterly,* 1, 45.

Fisher, R.A. (1950). *Statistical Methods of Research Workers.* New York : Hafner Publishing Co.

Garai, J. & Scheinfeld, A. (1968). Sex differences in mental and behavioural traits. *Genetic Psychology Monographs,* 77, 169-299.

Garcia, R.M. (1985). Achievement motivation, femininity traits and self-concept as characteristics of university women enrolled in professional career programmes in two selected universities. *Dissertation Abstracts International,* 46(2).

Gove, W. (1972). The relationship between sex-roles, marital status and mental illness. *Social Forces,* 51, 34-44.

Gove, W. & Tudor, J. (1973). Adult sex-role and mental illness. *American Journal of Sociology,* 78, 812-835.

Gysbers, N.C. & Johnston, J.A. (1968). Characteristics of homemaker and career oriented women. *Journal of Counselling Psychology,* 15(6), 541-546.

Hacker, H.M. (1971). The feminine protest to the working wife. *Indian Journal of Social Work,* 31.

Hilgard, E. & Atkinson, R. (1967). *Introduction to Psychology.* 4th ed. New York : Harcourt, Brace and World.

Hoffman, L.W. (1963). Paternal power relations and the Division of household tasks. In F.I. Nye & L.W. Hoffman (Eds.) *The Employed Mother in America.* Chicago : Rand McNally.

Hoffman, L.W. (1972). Early childhood experiences and women's achievement motives. *Journal of Social Issues,* 28(2), 129-150.

Hoffman, M.L. (1977). Personality and social psychology. *Annual Review of Psychology,* 28, 295-321.

Holahan, C.K. & Gilbert, L.A. (1979). Inter-role conflict for working women: Careers *versus* Jobs. *Journal of Applied Psychology,* 64(1), 86-90.

Horner, M.S. (1968). Sex differences in achievement motive and performance in competitive and non-competitive situations. Unpublished Doctoral Dissertations, The University of Michigan.

Horner, M.S. (1969). Fail : Bright Women. *Psychology Today,* 3(6), 36-38.

Horner, M.S. (1972). Toward an understanding of achievement related conflicts in women. *Journal of Social Issues,* 28, 157-176.

Hoyt. D. & Kennedy, C. (1958). Interest and personality correlates of career-motivated and home-making-motivated college women. *Journal of Counselling Psychology,* 5, 44-48.

James, W. (1890). *Principles of Psychology,* New York: Holt.

Joshi, P.; Garon, L. & Lechasseur, S. (1984). Self-esteem and loneliness among unemployed women. *Psychological Reports,* 54, 903-906.

Kanter, R. (1975). Women and the structure of organizations: Explorations in theory and behaviour. pp. 34-74 in Mareia Millman and Rosabeth Moss Kanter (Eds.), *Another Voice, Garden City,* New York: Anchor Books.

Kapur, P. (1974). *Marriage and the Working Women in India.* Vikas Publishing House, Pvt. Ltd., New Delhi.

Keith, P.M. & Schafer, R.B. (1980). Depression in one and two job families. *Psychological Reports,* 47(2), 669-670.

Keith, P.M. & Schafer, R.B. (1982). Correlates of depression among single parent, employed women. *Journal of Divorcee,* 5(3), 49-59.

Kerlinger, F.N. (1964). *Foundations of Behavioural Research : Educational and Psychological Inquiry,* New Yorsk, USA: Holt Rinehart and Winston Inc.

Komarovsky, M. (1946). Cultural contradictions and sex-roles. *American Journal of Sociology,* 52, 182-189.

Lesser, G.S.; Krawitz, R.N. & Packard, R. (1963). Experimental arousal of achievement motivation in adolescent girls. *Journal of Abnormal and Social Psychology,* 66, 59-66.

Lewis, E.C. (1968). *Developing Women's Potential.* Ames, Iowa: Iowa State University Press.

Lipman-Blumen, J. (1972). How ideology shapes women's lives. *Scientific American,* 226, 34-42.

Mackie, M. (1983). The domestication of self : Gender comparisons of self-imagery and self-esteem. *Social Psychology Quarterly,* 46(4), 343-350.

Marecek, J. & Ballon, D.J. (1981). Family roles and women's mental health. *Professional Psychology,* 12, 39-45.

Mason, K.O.; Czajka, J.L. & Arber, S. (1976). Change in U.S. women's sex-role attitudes. *American Sociological Review,* 41, 573-596.

Matter, D.E. (1982). Achievement motivation scores and biographical variables associated with marital status of high school graduates (1907–1967). *Psychological Reports,* 50(3), 1231-1236.

McClelland, D.C.; Atkinson, J.W.; Clark, R.A. & Lowell, E.L. (1953). *The Achievement Motive,* New York: Appleton-Century Crofts.

McKenzie, S.P. (1972). A comparative study of feminine role perceptions, selected personality characteristics and traditional attitudes of professional women and housewives. *Dissertation Abstracts International,* 32(10), 5615 A.

McManis, D.L. (1956). Pursuit rotor performance of normal and retarded children in four verbal-incentive conditions. *Child Development,* 36, 667-683.

Mead, G.H. (1934). *Mind, Self and Society.* Chicago : Univ. Chicago Press.

Montague, A. (1954). *The Natural Superiority of Women.* London, George Allen and Unwin Ltd.

Moorthy, V.M. (1945). Problems and welfare of our women workers. *Indian Journal of Social Work.* September.

More, D.M. & Suchner, R.W. (1976). Occupational status, prestige and stereotypes. *Sociology of Work and Occupations,* 3, 169-186.

Moriarty, A. (1961). Coping patterns of preschool children in response to intelligence test demands. *Genetic Psychology Monographs,* 64, 3-127.

Miner, J. (1965). *Studies in Management Education,* New York: Springer.

Murray, H. (1938). *Explorations in Personality.* New York: Oxford University Press.

Newcomb, T.M. *et al.* (1965). *Social Psychology.* New York: Holt, Rinehart and Winston, Inc.

Nye, F.I. (1974). Effects on mothers. In L.W. Hoffman & F.I. Nye (Eds.) *Working Mothers.* San Francisco: Jossery-Bass Publishers.

Oakley, A. (1974a). *The Sociology of House Work.* New York : Pantheon Book.

Oakley, A. (1974b). *Woman's Work : The Housewife Past and Present.* New York : Vintage Books.

Oetzel, R.M. (1966). Annotated bibliography and classified summary of research in sex differences. In E.E. Maccoby (Ed.) *The Development of Sex-differences.* Standford, California: Standford University Press.

Pathak, C.C. (1974). A study of achievement motive, educational norms and school performance. Unpublished Doctoral Dissertation, Sardar Patel University.

Phadke, M. & Kulkarni, A.V. (1977). Field-dependence-independence and employed-not-employed as factors in the adjustment of housewives. *Indian Journal of Psychology,* 52(1), 85-91.

Powers, S. & Sanchez, V. (1982). Correlates of Self-esteem of Mexican American Adolescents. *Psychological Reports,* 51, 771-774.

Prashant, A. (1988). Psychological stress in adolescents: A study of depression, self-esteem and physical symptoms. Doctoral Thesis (Unpublished), Banaras Hindu University.

Rao, U.M. (1976). A sociological study of occupational choices of under-graduate girls students. *Indian Journal of Social Work,* 37, 3-11.

Robbins, L. *et al.* (1983). Achievement motivation in medical students. *Journal of Medical Education,* 58(11), 850-858.

Robinson, G.; Erlick, P.M. & Brune, S. (1982). Autonomy in mothers with careers. *Canadian Journal of Psychiatry,* 27(4), 270-274.

Rosenberg, M. (1965). *Society and Adolescent Self-Image.* Princeton: Princeton University Press.

Rosenkrantz, P.S.; Vogel, S.R.; Bee, H.; Broverman, I.K. & Broverman, D.M. (1968). Sex-role stereotypes and self-concepts in college students. *Journal of Consulting and Clinical Psychology,* 32, 287-295.

Rossi, A.S. (1964). *Equality between the Sexes : An Immodest Proposal.* Daedalus, 93, 607-652.

Rossi, A.S. (1968). Transitions to parenthood. *Journal of Marriage and the Family*, 30, 26-39.

Ruddel, H. *et al.* (1982). Age group and sex specific differences of indicator values for personality characteristics (in the sense of Murray's personality) in a medium sized German City. *Psychologie*, 14(3), 253-261.

Sharp, L.J. (1963). Maternal mental health. In F.I. Nye & L.W. Hoffman (Eds.) *The Employed Mother in America.* Chicago: Rand McNally.

Shaver, P. & Freedman, J. (1976). Your pursuit of happiness. *Psychology Today*, 10, 26-32.

Shelton, P.B. (1968). Achievement motivation in professional women. *Dissertation Abstracts International*, 28, 427 A.

Shibutani, T. (1961). *Society and Personality.* Englewood Cliffs, N.J. : Prentice Hall.

Simpson, R.L. and Simpson, I.H. (1961). Occupational choice among career-oriented college women. *Marriage and Family Living*, 23, 377–383.

Stein, A.H. (1971). The effects of sex-role standards for achievement and sex-role preference on three determinants of achievement motivation. *Developmental Psychology*, 4, 219-231.

Stromberg, A.H. & Harkess, S. (1978). *Women Working* (Eds.) Palo Alto, Calif: Mayfield.

Terpstra, D.E. (1983). An investigation of job-seeker preferences through multiple methodologies. *Journal of Employment Counselling*, 20(4), 169-178.

Tripathi, R.R. (1973). *Manual for Aap Ki Pasand : Ek Anusoochi (Tripathi Personal Preference Schedule).* Varanasi : Raghuvir Sharan Publications.

Tyler, L. (1965). *The Psychology of Human Differences.* 2nd Ed. New York: Appleton-Century-Crofts.

Veroff, J. (1969). Social comparison and the development of achievement motivation. In C.P. Smith (Ed.), *Achievement Related Motives in Children*, New York : Russell Sage.

Veroff, J. ; Wilcox, S. & Atkinson, J.W. (1953). The achievement motive in high school and college women. *Journal of Abnormal and Social Psychology,* 48, 108–119.

Vogel, S.R.; Broverman, I.K; Broverman, D.M; Clarkson, F.E. & Rosenkrantz, P.S. (1970). Maternal employment and perception of sex-roles among college students. *Developmental Psychology,* 3, 384-391.

Von der Velden, H G M. (1974). An investigation into morbidity in housewives. *General Practice International,* 3, 123-127.

Walberg, H.J. (1969). Physics, femininity and creativity. *Developmental Psychology,* 1, 47-54.

Walker, L.J.S. & Walker, J.L. (1980). Trait anxiety in mothers: Differences associated with employment status, family size and age of children. *Psychological Reports,* 47, 295-299.

Welch, S. & Booth, A. (1977). Employment and health among married women and children. *Sex Roles : A Journal of Research,* 3, 385-398.

Wells, L.E. & Marwell, G. (1976). *Self-esteem: Its Conceptualization and Measurement.* Beverly Hills : Sage.

White, M.S. (1970). Psychological and social barriers to women in science. *Science,* 170, 413-416.

Winterbottom, M.R. (1958). The relation of need for achievement to learning experience in independence and mastery. In J.W. Atkinson (Ed) *Motives in Fantasy : Action and Society.* Princeton, N.J. : Van Nostrand.

Wylie, R.C. (1974). *The Self-Concept.* Lincoln, N.E. ; Univ. Nebraska Press. Vol. 1.

Yuen, R.K ; Tinsley, D.J. & Howard, J. (1980). The vocational needs and background characteristics of home-maker-oriented women and career oriented women. *Vocational Guidance Quarterly,* 28(3), 250-256.

Index